Sellers on Sellers

Sellers on Sellers

Michael Sellers
and Gary Morecambe

Additional material Maxine Ventham

ANDRE DEUTSCH

First published in Great Britain in 2000
by André Deutsch Limited
76 Dean Street W1V 5HA
www.vci.co.uk

A catalogue record for this book is available from the British Library.

ISBN 0 233 99883 7

Jacket and book design by Roger Hammond

Printed in Italy

1 3 5 7 9 10 8 6 4 2

Contents

Acknowledgements

Numerous are those who help in the preparation of such a book as this, and to all those mentioned throughout these pages, the authors are truly grateful. A particular thanks goes to Roy Boulting, Marjorie Graham, Sandra Skuse, John Scheinfeld and The George Brown Collection. And a special thank you to all those who contributed a memory of Peter. Without you, there would be no book. Finally, thanks to all at Deutsch – especially Ingrid Connell – who have shown great patience and imagination. And thanks to our agent, Jennifer Luithlen; the lass from Leicester doing her stuff as usual.

A Chronology

1925   Born Richard Henry Sellers 8 September
at Southsea.

1941   Joins ENSA (entertainment shows in wartime Britain) with
his father.

1943   With the RAF in India.

1945   Tours with David Lodge and Dennis Selinger. (Peter plays
drums.)

1948   Appearance on BBC TV's *New To You*. Appears at the
Windmill Theatre. First appearance on *Variety Bandbox*.

1949   First series of *Ray's A Laugh*. (Peter stayed until 1954,
overlapping *The Goon Show*.)

1951   Film – *Penny Points to Paradise*. BBC Radio transmits
first of *The Goon Show*.

1951   Marries Anne Hayes.

1953   First record – 78rpm: *Jakka and the Flying Saucers* (*An
Interplanetary Tale*). Peter dubs for Humphrey Bogart in
film – *Beat The Devil*.

1951. Anne Hayes

1954   Acting role in film *Orders Are Orders* featuring Sid James.

1954   Peter's son, Michael, is born on 2 April.

1956   Film – *The Ladykillers* with Alec Guinness and
Herbert Lom. *A Show Called Fred* and *Son of
Fred* with Spike Milligan. Two chart hits: *I'm
Walking Backwards for Christmas* and *The
Ying Tong Song*, both with the Goons.

1954. Michael born

Opposite: *Peter, Spike and Harry – the Goons. The show ran from 1951 to 1960*

Opposite: *1964.*
Blake Edwards
and Peter on the
set of The Pink
Panther

1957	First solo chart hit: *Any Old Iron.*
1957	Peter's daughter, Sarah, is born on 16 October.
1958	Film – *tom thumb.* First LP: *The Best of Sellers.* Play: *Brouhaha* directed by Peter Hall.
1959	The Boulting Brothers establish Peter as an actor in the film – *I'm All Right, Jack.*
1960	Film – *The Millionairess* with Sophia Loren. Develops an infatuation with her.
1961	Peter directs himself for the only time in film – *Mr Topaze.*
1962	Film – Stanley Kubrick's *Lolita.* Guest appearance with Bob Hope and Bing Crosby in *Road to Hong Kong.*
1962	Father dies of heart attack, aged 62.
1963	Divorces Anne Hayes.
1964	Film – Blake Edwards's *The Pink Panther.* Stanley Kubrick's film – *Dr Strangelove.* Peter's three diverse roles earn him an Oscar nomination for the latter.
1964	Marries Britt Ekland.
1964	First heart attacks.
1964	Film – *A Shot in the Dark*
1965	Film – *What's New, Pussycat?*
1966	Peter's daughter, Victoria, is born on 20 January.
1966	Created a CBE.
1967	Mother dies aged 72.
1968	Divorces Britt Ekland.
1968	Film – *The Party.*

1966. Victoria born

1964. Peter and Britt
on their wedding day

1962. With Kennedy and Macmillan

1969   BBC TV documentary *Will the Real Peter Sellers...*
        Narrated by Spike Milligan.

1970   Marries Miranda Quarry.

1971   Film – *There's a Girl in my Soup.*

1972   *The Last Goon Show of All.*

1973   Has high-profile affair with Liza Minnelli.

1974   Film – *The Optimists of Nine Elms.*

1974   Marriage to Miranda Quarry is dissolved.

1975   Film – *The Return of the Pink Panther.*

1976   Film – *Pink Panther Strikes Again.*

1977   Marries Lynne Frederick in Paris.

1978   Film – *The Revenge of the Pink Panther.*

1979   Last LP – *Sellers Market.* Film – *Being There.* For
        his role, he receives his second academy award
        nomination.

1980   Film – *The Fiendish Plot of Dr Fu
        Manchu.*

1980   Dies of heart attack in London.

1973. Peter with Liza Minnelli

*1980. As Fu Manchu
in his last film*

Clouseau with bent skis, delighting a crowd

Introduction

the year 2000 marks the twentieth anniversary of **Peter Sellers' death.** He was to comic acting what Laurence Olivier was to straight acting. He is revered by a new generation of comedians and comic actors, such as American superstar Robin Williams, who describes his idol as '...the Master!'

Peter would have been seventy-five in September – the age at which he *should* have died according to a spiritualist he met in the RAF during the Second World War. In his early fifties, when his health was declining, it was his recurrent thought – and hope – that he might have two decades yet to live. It was not to be. He died just short of his fifty-fifth birthday in 1980.

Peter Sellers was one of my greatest heroes. Through his work I embraced a new form of comedy, which added to the comedy of my upbringing – namely Morecambe and Wise. I was hooked on

Opposite:

Peter in 1964

Sellers' talent from an early age, and the comic uniqueness of Peter Sellers fills a large part of my memories of childhood and youth.

There are two Sellers films which have touched me like no films before or since. The first is *The Party* (1968). In it, Sellers gives a virtuoso performance as Hrundi V. Bakshi, an Indian guest at a party to which he is accidentally invited. Back before it was politically incorrect to do so, it was said of Asian Indians that they sounded like Peter Sellers!

My second Sellers film favourite is arguably one of the greatest films ever made: *Being There* (1979). Sellers had wanted to make *Being There* ever since reading the novel by Jerzy Kosinski some seven years earlier. The hero of the piece, and the role Sellers was to play, is Chance Gardiner. He's never set foot outside the walled garden at the home of the millionaire whose lawns and plants he tends. He has only experienced the 'real world' through the endless watching of television. Through frankness, honesty, naïvety and a regurgitation of things he has seen on television – by doing no more than 'being there' – he goes from tending a garden to being one of the President of the United States's closest allies and, himself, a potential President in waiting. Like Chance, Sellers, too, had become a celebrity beyond his own comprehension and was thus able to relate to this character more so than the many others he had played.

In the many words that have been written about him since his

death, there has been a deliberate focus on the bleak side. His son,
Michael, is quick to point out that while there certainly was a bleak
side, things weren't always as black as they have been painted.
While clearly selfish and almost childish at times, and allowing his
life to become governed by superstitions and morbid thoughts,
making him a frequently disappointed and disappointing figure,
Sellers is still done an injustice by being portrayed solely as a dark,
brooding monster. Until having the opportunity of meeting
Michael, it was the only image I had been sold of the private
Peter Sellers.

G.M. SOMERSET 2000

Overleaf: *Peter the car enthusiast, in a Mercedes*

MICHAEL SELLERS

1

On 24 July 1980, Alan Whicker announced on BBC1 in solemn tones to the nation that Peter Sellers had died. As I watched I thought, even this I must share: but then, it was usually through the media that I found out what my father was doing at any given time.

ON PETER SELLERS

Of the many attempts to chronicle the life of Peter Sellers, few have come close to the man behind the image and only Peter Evans had input from my father. While this book is not a biography, I hope that the memories of his family and friends might offer some insight into the real Peter Sellers.

My father was a simple man in a complicated world. He had a unique, chameleon-like ability to become the person he was talking to or the character he was playing. He often said there was no Peter Sellers. But I knew that there was because I could always tell when he was absent. But to define that in words would be like describing a photograph over the telephone.

He was definitely a tormented man. He had to sleep with the

man he was, and the weight of a self-centred life finally caught up with him.

The last time I saw him, in July 1980, he looked used up. He had been there; starred in the movies; married the young women; driven the fast cars; taken the drugs; drunk the wine; made the cash; spent the cash and, less forgivably, let down all those people who had ever really cared for him.

I was born in 1954, my father's first and only son, with his first wife (of four), Anne Hayes. Despite the break-up of their marriage when I was only eight after my father developed an infatuation with the actress Sophia Loren, as a child I had a loving relationship with him. My sister Sarah, who was three years younger, had a more difficult time with him and as I got older and both our lives became more complicated, my father and I grew apart. The closest we came to each other as adults was at the very end of his life. During that time much was done to repair our damaged relationship.

Any retrospective on my father's life would include his four marriages and various liaisons with the opposite sex. But I will begin by going back a little earlier; before the wealth and fame and women had created a maelstrom from which he was never able to fully emerge.

From my standpoint, my father's story opens with his own parents, Bill and Peg. Bill actually died around the time my parents broke up, but Peg continued to play a part in our lives. I had a

Opposite:

Michael and

Victoria

Peter photographs his mother Peg

fairly good relationship with my paternal grandmother, but I could see her faults. She was a clinger and a very dominant lady. 'My dear, come and give me a hug – don't you love me any more? Hug me some more.' She was a short, dark woman, deceptively frail in appearance.

There were the times she would come to school to pick me up. She wouldn't wait in the car, but come to the main gates standing there in all her finery. We'd have to go through the full hugging routine on the steps of the school: not great for your street-cred.

In the beginning, Peg disliked my mother: this was because she disliked any female getting close to her only son. She considered them competitors, and she did her utmost to get rid of them, particularly my mother as that relationship had ended in marriage. Then I was born, and that was it – she had her grandson and she duly accepted my mother in her own strange way.

My father and Peg had a love-hate relationship – from *his* point of view, at least. He enjoyed winding her up. But if I think she smothered me, then she *really* smothered him when he was a child. It was a bit weird, to be honest. Not to the level of being incestuous, but it would make anyone on the outside feel very uncomfortable. She controlled his life. She may have been the one person he would actually listen to.

My mother doesn't really agree, but I firmly believe that when Peg died in 1967, that finally unleashed him on an unsuspecting world. He then had absolutely no authority to answer to. Peg would ring him and tell him he shouldn't be doing this that and the other, and he would at least listen and sometimes agree. After that there was nothing to hold him back. And he needed someone, because it's very easy to fall foul of your own publicity, especially when you have had an unusual and spoilt upbringing. Peg always told him he was wonderful and, as an adult, every one else was telling him he was wonderful. There was no levelling force in his life.

Most of my father's later superstitions stemmed from Peg. Never put keys on a table. If I give you a gift with a point you must give me a penny. The colours green and purple are unlucky. Don't talk about the Scottish play. All that type of thing. After she died, he used to burn a candle and have a picture of her by it, convinced she was present. It was probably his interest in Buddhism that prompted him to create a little shrine to his mother.

Many of his later problems stemmed from being thoroughly spoilt by Peg. His impetuosity – the need to buy something he wanted at that very instant, then being bored very quickly soon after. As children, we would be told we were going for a ride in his car, then he would change his mind and put it back in the garage. He would want to see us, or certain friends, call us round, then not want to see us. I am sure this stems from Peg indulging his every whim. 'No' was a foreign concept to her, and this was made worse by his being an only child.

When my father was a young lad he lived with his mother in Muswell Hill, North London. His father, Bill, lived down the road

Like father, like son. Peter and Mike at the première of The Return of the Pink Panther

at Holloway. This unusual set-up was taken for granted and never questioned or explained. It meant that there was no sense of family, something we also lacked a generation later, when he and my mother divorced. Bill was an easygoing man, but not a force in my father's life, which was a shame. It meant the only influence throughout his childhood and youth was Peg, and she was always pushing the image of, 'My son, the star!'

Following the divorce from our mother, he would often try and play us against each parent. 'Who do you love the most?' he

once asked. Sarah sensibly replied, 'You and Mummy equally.'
Being belligerent and generally pissed off, I immediately replied,
'Mummy!'

'You get out,' he shouted, 'and take all your stuff. I never want
to see you again. You are no longer my child.' It still seems to me
rather harsh treatment of an eight-year-old.

On that occasion, Peg tried to intercede, but he still sent us
packing. When we got back to my mother's, she told us that
apparently a truck was arriving containing everything that was
ours. I remember telling my mother, 'I hate him, I hate him,' which
I didn't, of course, but he was a hopeless case at times.

My mother said much the same thing, adding, 'It'll be all right
in time,' which it usually was.

And he never apologized for his behaviour. When we spoke
some time later, he carried on as if nothing had ever happened.
And it was not the last time he would fly off the handle in that
manner.

My sister Sarah had a different relationship with our father.
She was more like him and wouldn't put up with his temperament.
They therefore didn't have a particularly close relationship, not
helped by the fact she was a girl and didn't share any of his
interests. For me, at least I shared his love of cars and the gadgets.
Poor Sarah always came off second best. But there was very little I
could have done about that. I had to progress through that
minefield myself, which was difficult enough.

Peter with Victoria
on the set of
I Love You, Alice
B. Toklas

Living in that 'minefield' was the main reason why I eventually found myself at boarding school. My mother saw it as the best means to get me away from an unsettling upbringing.

As a youngster I was the apple of his eye – the son and heir of whom he was so proud. My mother has often said to me that she doesn't know what happened and when, but suddenly he turned off.

When I speak to someone like Hattie Stephenson, who was my father's secretary for a while, she says that in the 1960s, when first separated from my mother, he would go on all the time about getting us, the kids, over to see him. Five minutes after we'd arrived, he'd say, 'Get rid of them.' We were too much effort for him, so he sent us home. Typical of his impetuosity, really. Want that, have that – don't want that now, get rid of it! As a maxim, it can be applied to almost everything in life that attracted him.

My father was certainly unpredictable. I can't say whether or not that came from Peg. It probably had more to do with his gift for comedy and his ability to become a different person every second. He'd ring me up and if he'd say, 'Hello, Mike,' I knew it was fine. If it was a sterner, 'Hello, Michael?' then I knew there was some rubbish to come down the line at me. But I could read him very easily. Apparently, according to my mother, at as young as eight years old I was already humouring him.

During my years at boarding school, I'd see my father every other weekend if he was in the country and during the holidays, of course. By the time I'd finished with school – I would have been

sixteen or seventeen – my father and I had some good times
together. We would often have Sunday lunch at San Lorenzo's in
Wimbledon. Sometimes we'd be joined by Sammy Davies or Liza
Minnelli. 'Number One Son,' was how he referred to me, as in
Charlie Chan. We did a lot of Goon dialogue together. The
Bloodnoks: that type of thing. When I was seventeen I was
working in a hi-fi shop when my father rang up. He'd been
commissioned to photograph a hotel in Acapulco and wanted to
know if I'd like to go to Mexico with him for three weeks. 'Yes,' I
said instantly. 'When do we go?' 'Tomorrow,' he said casually.
This was typical of him, though our holidays together didn't always
go smoothly.

One summer, in the late 60s, we agreed to meet up in Venice. I
reached the airport and the first thing I found was Miranda Quarry
(his third wife) in tears and on her way back to England. There
had obviously been a big row, and she'd been thrown out.
Following this hello-goodbye, I got to my father's boat.

'Oh, hello, Mike. Enjoy it, I'm off now.'

I'd gone all the way to Venice, taking a boat down the canals
to find where he was moored, got all my luggage out of a taxi, to
be greeted in this 'farewell' manner. He then proceeded to take
my taxi!

'I'll be back later,' he called out, then was gone – for good!

I went from Venice all the way round to Monaco on his boat –
just me and the crew. I had a brilliant time; it was quite an

education! Perhaps things hadn't worked out so badly after all.

Perhaps because we were always emulating them, Moriarty (played by Spike Milligan) and Herculees Grytpype-Thynne (played by my father) were my favourite Goon characters. The idea was that Grytpype originally came across Moriarty before the Second World War, at which time he was a suave Count who was to be seen with all the right people on the Côte d'Azur. Grytpype was, however, a con-man with an English military style. Post war, Moriarty fell on hard times, and was systematically reduced to the bedraggled, cringing aide of Grytpype in the Goon shows.

Whenever we arrived at any new port in the yacht, we were on the look-out for evidence of those two Goon characters, Grytpype-Thynne and the impoverished Moriarty, whom we pretended would have the tattiest boat in the harbour, which was usually tucked away in a corner and half submerged. If it floated, they could be heard at night after dinner going amongst the yachts calling, 'New bones for old!' in an effort to gain some nourishment from newly discarded scraps.

Grytpype always had extended titles for Moriarty such as, Count Knees Moriarty French, overland saxaphone champion of 1933. Or, Count Sprockets Moriarty of Katmandu, the pioneer film-maker. Of course, Grytpype was well placed to introduce him, and would happily invite him, on your behalf, to the party. The Count, who was unable to attend, had sent Grytpype in his stead, but would sneak in and hide beneath the table awaiting morsels to be passed to him. But in time, hunger would get the better of him, and a hand would appear from below the table. Grytpype would immediately swat the hand, and an agonized noise could be heard from below.

It was a game my father and I invented – or lifted – from the Goons. I would sit across the table from him, and bring my hand slowly up over the edge. My father would then swat it, and we both would make the noise. You've got to say, 'OW!'

Character voices were one thing, but if I ever said something with a cockney accent, he would jump on my elocution. It reminded him of his upbringing, his background, and became common to him. But he could use rhyming slang very amusingly. He'd nudge me and say, 'What do you think of the Richards?' (Richard the Thirds – Birds.) That type of thing. It was certainly lost on girls in the South of France.

Once we went into a car park in his Ferrari. A woman pulled up in a Morris, too close for his liking; he was worried she was going to bump into his car. As we got out, she started to stare, and you could see in her face that she had recognized him. So he turned to Bert, his chauffeur, and said, 'Did you tie that dynamite down properly?'

'Yeah, I think it's all right,' said Bert who, like others, had learned that when my father went for it, you just go with him. 'So long as it doesn't get shaken too much.'

The woman's expression gradually changed. Dynamite. Car.

Without a word, she got back in and moved away to another parking place.

He had bought the Ferrari as a gift for Britt Eckland, his second wife, but when he tried it out, he liked it so much he kept it for himself!

He always showed appreciation to anyone who came up and wanted to shake his hand. What he hated was having to stop and do autographs – and it was never for them but for someone they knew, like a poor crippled aunt in hospital who had just had her head removed. 'What's her name?'

'John!'

'Yeah, right. OK.'

You could never go anywhere on foot with him without being stopped. A handshake is relatively easy, but signing bits of paper isn't.

There's a plaque on a house somewhere in Portsmouth where he was born, above what is now a fish and chip shop. Someone came up to him saying, 'Peter Sellers, how are you? What brings you to these parts?'

'I was born here.'

'Oh, right. I love that *Shot in the Dark* film, and the way that fella jumps through a window...'

'Yes,' interrupted my father, 'it's a shame though, he died doing that!'

'You what?'

'Yes. He fell out the window and broke his back on the pond. What a shame!'

He loved winding people up. Sometimes he did so without realizing it. When he was into the Indian transcendental meditation thing that became very cultish in the late 1960s following the Beatles' infamous trips to India, he once cleared the first-class lounge of a jumbo jet because he insisted on standing on his head to meditate!

But lifts were definitely the place where he was at his most naughty. He would stand in a busy lift a moment, then start going into gruesome detail about a totally fictitious event. 'Did you see what they did to that fella in the lobby? There was blood coming out of his head,' and so on, just telling us what he'd witnessed as a passer-by. The other people in the lift would look really concerned and wouldn't know whether to laugh, cry or ignore it.

Then there was a scene from a Panther film, which the writer and presenter Denis Norden made famous. The fart scene in the lift, as it became affectionately known! My father and the other cast were crammed inside a lift waiting for the director's cue for 'action'. Unfortunately the cue sounded like a fart, so over countless takes, the cast fell about laughing instead of taking it as the cue for action.

Peter Sellers' ability as a mimic is legendary, notably gaining him his first break in 1948 on a radio programme called *Showtime*. It was produced by Roy Speer and compered by Dick Bentley.

Having unsuccessfully tried to get a booking, he decided to call
Roy Speer using the voice of *Round the Horne's* Kenneth Horne.
The secretary taking the call recognized Horne's voice and put him
through. My father, in the guise of Horne, said that he and Dickie
Murdoch (comedian) had seen this wonderful new talent the night
before, and that he should book him right away. His name was
Peter Sellers. Speer agreed and started writing this down. 'Actually,
I *am* Peter Sellers,' confessed my father. Speer was flabbergasted.
'What do you do?' he asked. 'Well, impressions for a start,' replied
my father. After a telling off, he was given the booking.

   Less well known is the fact that during the earlier part of his
career, he once dubbed Humphrey Bogart's voice. It was in the

'*I am the sum of the parts I have played,*' my father said, adding once, *jokingly,* that there was no real Peter Sellers because he had had it surgically removed.

film *Beat the Devil* (1953). Apparently, Bogey wasn't available for overdubs. It would be interesting to see if the impersonation can be spotted.

His versatility enabled him to do this voice-over work. In *Malaga* (1954) my father voiced fourteen parts including eleven of the characters conversing together in one scene! In *The Man Who Never Was* (1955) he was the voice of Sir Winston Churchill, and in *Our Girl Friday* (1953) he was the parrot!

It was on 28 May 1951 that for Peter Sellers voice-overs and impersonations for producers could be finally discarded. *Those Crazy People* took to the airwaves. Thirteen months later they were re-named the Goons, and continued to entertain on the radio until 1960. I was born in 1954, right in the middle of their madcap life.

It was immediately after the war that my father had met this group of ex-servicemen entertainers with shared war time experiences. Harry Secombe, Spike Milligan, Michael Bentine and Peter would get together in a pub near Victoria, London and work out comic ideas. Spike was the real nutter – always was and still is.

I've always loved Spike's comedy. His mind comes from somewhere different from most people's – he just cuts across what you are thinking.

An early memory of mine is my father encouraging me to repeat the phrase, 'He's fallen in the water.' Goon show addicts will know it well. I originally came out with the line at the age of three when at Spike's house watching him leap into his swimmingpool. With Bluebottle, Eccles et al as role models, it's a wonder I take the real world seriously.

I went to see *The Last Goon Show Of All* (1972) being recorded and sat in on the script meets and rehearsals. It was interesting to see how it all revolved around Spike and how, unusually for my father, he stood back for him. After Spike and the Goons he never played a secondary role for anyone. He was a star, and that was how he always perceived himself. The Goon thing, had it continued, would have in any case gone out the window once my father took off in his own right.

But, if you're looking for clues to my father's character in his work, you'd have to go back to the Goons and Spike Milligan. He and Spike seemed to look at the world the same way. I think Spike understood my father better than anyone else. Spike, of course, had too many problems of his own to be a really beneficial influence on my father. He had nervous breakdowns and manic depression to deal with. In fact, I think my father spent more time helping Spike out of depression than Spike did sorting out *his* problems.

My father and Spike reprised their early lunacy, and after a good evening at the Trattoo restaurant, rounded it off by being driven about London, both sitting in the back of my father's Mercedes, wearing leather coats and Nazi helmets. They shouted out the windows at people in German-style jibberish, and saluted statues.

Reunited in 1972 for The Last Goon Show of All

I was talking to Spike at his house some time after my father's death. He said how much he missed him. My father had rung him up shortly before his death saying that they must get together 'because I want to laugh again'. That says a lot to me about where my father's life was at that time. Their particular brand of shared humour and fun had gone: nothing left was really funny to him any more.

If you look back to 1961–62, it seemed my father had all he could have possibly wanted. He was making films such as *Mister Topaze, The Millionairess* and *Lolita.* He had a beautiful wife who had willingly given up her own acting career to support his; a family; people throwing money at him from every direction; a twenty-seven room mansion in Hertfordshire. He had the lot. Yet it wasn't enough for him. He threw it away.

At one time he had a house in Elstead, Surrey – a huge spread. After he split up from Britt he sold it to Ringo Starr. By then he didn't really want a home base, somewhere to retreat. He couldn't handle it: he couldn't handle himself, alone, and away from the public glare. He didn't like his own company – he needed an audience, and he needed to be where things were happening.

These beautiful homes would end up as just a strain on his wallet. Enough of that house – let's get a new one. That was the way he thought.

The actor, the late Alfred Marks, a long-time friend of my father's, bought one of his North London houses from Peter. It was

a bit of an awkward occasion because, just before Alfred was due
to take possession, my father set fire to it!

It was Guy Fawkes night 1959, and a firework from the
garden shot through a door and ignited a whole box of fireworks
which were stored in the lounge. All of us were running in every
direction to escape these screaming, exploding things. Eventually,
my father got us all into the car, but discovered that the battery
was on charge. He undid the connecting leads, then shut the
bonnet trapping the edge of his coat.

'Mike. Pull the lever!' he called out.

'What lever, Dad?'

He started to try and take his coat off while still trapped by
the bonnet.

My mother quickly rang the fire brigade and said, 'Could you
come at once, because we have a fire in the house,' which amused
her enormously, as every house in the area had a fire in it!

It was Clouseau in the flesh! (In fact, a scene very similar
appeared in the first *Panther* film and I've often wondered if the
two were connected.)

Next morning my father gave Alfred a ring. 'Well, Alfred,' he
began. 'Everything's okay except for the lounge, which we burnt
down last night! But you can still have it on the agreed date.'

Even now whenever I smell something burning, I'm at once
transported back to that night.

Tommy Sopwith, the aviator, once turned up at our Brookfield

home in a helicopter one summer while my father was recovering from a heart attack. We all rushed out into the field with white sheets for markers.

At Tommy's suggestion, we took a ride. We thought it a fun idea to drop in – literally – on some friends living a few miles away. My father made a minor navigational error, and we landed in an elderly couple's garden during their afternoon tea. They were somewhat bemused at the sight of Peter Sellers coming towards them out of a helicopter with a request for directions!

Success clearly changed my father. When we lived a more humble existence in North London, he was a plumper, more straightforward human being making a good, if not extraordinary, career as a comic actor.

Then he was more the father and the family man before the pretensions of being some kind of dashing matinee idol struck deep in his imagination. And it was a way of life he seemed convincingly comfortable with. But with fame and success family life and fatherhood became no more than a passing role.

Tommy Sopwith's helicopter arrives at Brookfield on a visit to Peter

Even back in those early days, he had a temper of which I was very afraid. Although the first eight years of my life seemed a relatively normal family upbringing, there were still mood swings and arguments to blot the landscape.

It was waking up at night to hear my parents fighting that I hated the most. I was about four or five. Their room backed on to mine, so there was no getting away from his shouting and my mother's crying.

The actor, David Lodge, was always a part of our family, but never more so than in those days. David, who is also my godfather, used to come to the house and end up protecting us from my father. He was Uncle Dave, the man who would always intervene. It was him and not my father who read me a bedtime story. Though protective of us, he always remained a faithful friend to my father.

We needed Dave, because my father's anger was like a self-perpetuating fire – he'd just go loopier and loopier – very much the archetypal 'mad genius'.

My father could never be happy with the stability of a home and family life. In the early days of his career, his work took him abroad half the year and he was effectively able to lead a double life. But that wasn't enough. When he became dissatisfied with something, he had to completely discard it and move on to something new. He had a boat in the Mediterranean for years, but he even tired of that and got rid of it.

In 1960, he saw a manor house at Chipperfield in Hertfordshire advertised in the *Sunday Times* and decided he had to have that. He remarked of the move, 'I wanted a place I could walk around without crossing any streets. It is a very civilized exile.'

But, if anything, Chipperfield suffocated him. He found its isolation more claustrophobic than the street-housing of his humble past.

As someone adept at playing roles, he fancied the part of Squire, right down to the plus fours and deer-stalker. The one role he couldn't handle was that of being himself. 'I am the sum of the parts I have played,' was what he said. He even once joked that there was no real him because he had had it surgically removed!

There is an element of truth in what he said. Whatever he was playing at a given moment, *that* is who he was. As a performer, he could be like a machine – feed the information in and out would come the character plus a great deal more: a bonus for most directors, but a strain on the real person within.

The director Stanley Kubrick said that when Sellers had a sudden bite of inspiration and went off in that direction, if you didn't go with him, you lost it: you couldn't get him to repeat it. He was very spontaneous in that way. From what I've heard from other people, this was indeed the case – he could never repeat; never 'take' again for the cameras. If he fluffed a line, then he would say, 'I've fluffed my line,' but he could never do an exact re-take; it was always different.

Peter joking with Sophia Loren and Max Geldray

Stanley Kubrick understood totally. As Kubrick said, 'I always shot Peter with three cameras, because I couldn't go back and get the repeat from the other angle.'

This spontaneity was one of the reasons he tired of live theatre performance. Theatre required him to be the same character every night, saying exactly the same words and doing exactly the same actions. On film, he would do the given part in various ways and when that was done it would be on to the next scene or role.

The talent for improvisation was something he shared with Blake Edwards, who he teamed up with for the Pink Panther films. With the character of Inspector Clouseau, they clicked, wound each other up and went for it. Blake would try to be more contrived at times, which was the usual source of their arguments. My father preferred the comedy to develop naturally and not become reliant on props and sets that moved, which was moving towards farce. In moments during the last of the Panther movies, it can be seen that Blake had clearly got his way.

The Panthers, though not by design, were made in two batches – 1964 was *The Pink Panther* followed by *A Shot In The Dark*; 1975–78 was *The Return of the Pink Panther*, *The Pink Panther Stikes Again* and, finally, *Revenge of the Pink Panther.* By the second film of the latter batch of releases, my father had become bored with the whole Panther business. It was the repetition he couldn't take. They wanted to pay him large amounts

Blake Edwards (left) and David Niven (right) are discussing a serious point.

Peter (with one of his beloved cameras) is clearly amused by something else

of money to do it, but he wouldn't go for it with Blake: to make another one, it had to be done some other way. So he co-wrote a script himself with a man called Jim Maloney. Clive Donner was signed to direct, and the main reason why my father was at the Dorchester in London at the time of his sudden death was to interview for a potential leading lady for this movie; Pamela Stephenson being the hot favourite. Of course, it was never to be.

The first time Peter Sellers and Blake Edwards crossed paths was on the orginal Panther in 1964. In the beginning, Peter Ustinov was up for the part of Clouseau, and my father was up for the part which Ustinov was to play in the film *Topkapi.* For some reason the roles got swopped: Ustinov and Sellers got along very well. They'd made a record together at the time of the first Panther called, sensibly enough, *The Two Peters.*

Blake and my father also hit it off when they got to Rome to discuss the character of Clouseau. Their ideas at once clicked, and all credit to Blake who had a cast that included David Niven, Robert Wagner, Capucine and Claudia Cardinale. He realized straight away that they were on to something big if the Clouseau role were written up. The original idea was that Clouseau, the French detective, would be a 'bit' part. By the time they were set to shoot, they had reshaped the movie around Clouseau. As a young boy on the set, drifting around watching film history in the making, no less, I had a wonderful experience to look back on.

The Panther movie was always going to be a comedy caper.

But Blake discovered he had a better film to be made than was originally planned.

A Shot in the Dark remains my favourite of the Panther films. It was also the film which introduced Herbert Lom as his long suffering superior. And all the time the Clouseau idiosyncrasies were being developed. By the time my father reprised the role for the last outing in 1978, it had peaked. There was nowhere further to take it: it had become repetitive and very self-indulgent, but at the beginning it had been exciting to watch it happen.

It was similar with Stanley Kubrick. When working with my father on *Dr Strangelove* (1964), he soon realized how to maximize the potential of Peter Sellers. He didn't take on a character and become confined within four walls, he just went, and as long as you hung on to the coat tails, you went with it, because the character grew and grew: there was no defined limit as to where he could go with a character. That was Peter Sellers' gift.

Stanley Kubrick and Peter concentrating on Dr Strangelove, 1964

The problems for Peter Sellers the man really began when he became a superstar. Suddenly there were people running around after him, nothing was too difficult for him. For a man lacking in self-control, it was a dangerous position to be in. On a film set he was given too much power and control and would throw tantrums. Sometimes he wouldn't appear for a scene. David Lodge, with whom he worked on many occasions, would go over to him and say, 'Well, what should I do?' My father would reply, 'Keep getting paid until I'm ready to shoot the scene!'

David would be kept hanging around on full pay. The director would then say, 'OK, let's shoot a different scene, then.'

'I don't want to shoot a different scene,' my father would say. 'But I might want to shoot *this* scene tomorrow.'

David would be embarrassed that he was hanging around being paid good money when he should have been working.

Though David always kept a watchful eye on my father, the more famous and outrageous Peter Sellers became, the less able he was to do so. He didn't exactly ditch his old friends, he just saw less of them. Suddenly he was a big star out in Hollywood, losing sight of what he really was and where he had come from.

My father was invited to New York for promotion of *The Mouse That Roared* (1959). His first taste of film stardom American-style. He invited David Lodge to go, but Dave was busy, so he invited an old mucker, Graham Stark, and they both enjoyed

Cary Grant and

Peter, perched on

Peter's Rolls Royce

immense star-status hospitality. My mother then joined them for
the trip back to London on the Queen Elizabeth.

His star was now rapidly ascending and it showed in the
people he was starting to hang out with – names such as Cary
Grant, Warren Beatty and Sammy Davies Jnr. In the early
Seventies, whilst in L.A., I went with my father to the races at Cary
Grant's invitation. During the course of the day his friends had
been giving me tips. At one point I was doing quite well; that is
until I fancied a horse which, needless to say, didn't show. At the

Peter with one of his Minis – the car of the 60s

end of the meeting, we accompanied Cary Grant down to the winners' enclosure. As I walked with him the crowds parted, doors opened, people said, 'Good afternoon, Mr Grant,' and the jockeys all said eager 'hellos'. In his own way he too was Royalty – Hollywood Royalty. He took great pleasure in driving my father and me around old Hollywood, telling us stories about the early days out there, and showing us the extent of the original MGM lot.

Dad needed this celebrity 'friendship' to sustain the new matinee idol image he had created for himself: he had to be seen with the right people. And he ended up having a reputation equal to that of Warren Beatty's, which takes some doing, I imagine.

And yet, my father never fully let go of people and things from the past, as if sensing they represented a more sane time before the madness of success was thrust upon him. He had this curious nature whereby he would discard everything as he continued his journey through life, but then like to go back just to have a sneaky look. Not just friends, but old houses and theatres. He wanted to float among the ghosts of yesteryear. I don't know if there were specific occurrences which triggered this desire: he wasn't a particularly nostalgic man. Maybe it was just the disillusionment; that inner uncertainty over what he was before fame had taken him over. Or maybe he was just plain nosey, because he didn't limit himself to the distant past – he also enjoyed visiting the big homes he had once owned.

We first heard about this person called Britt Ekland when my father was just starting his second Panther movie, *A Shot in the Dark* (1964).

Sarah and I would visit him most weekends at the Dorchester Hotel in London, where he was staying during the filming. On about our third visit, he sat us down and told us he had some very special photos to show us. He produced some pictures of a blonde bombshell. 'Who do you think that is?' he asked us.

'Is she in the film with you, Dad?' I remember asking.

He once cleared the first-class lounge of a jumbo jet because he insisted on standing on his head to meditate!

'No, she's not,' he smiled. 'Her name is Britt Ekland and she comes from Sweden. Isn't she beautiful? How would you like Daddy to marry her?'

This question turned out to be rhetorical, as he'd already proposed to Britt by then. He had only known her a matter of days having first glimpsed her browsing through magazines in the hotel's foyer.

Only two months earlier, Maurice Woodruff, the clairvoyant he had consulted for some years, had told him he would shortly become involved with a person whose initials were B.E. Now he had found her and, despite the fact that Blake Edwards could lay claim to the same initials, he was convinced that this was the person Maurice had meant.

Maurice was a big influence on him. I think the poor man found it hard going dealing with Peter Sellers' foibles. He used to ring up my mother or Bert (Bert Mortimer – Sellers' chauffeur and general factotum) and say, 'What have I got to tell him this week? What direction are we pointing him in?'

Extravagant gifts always went with the early stages of his romances. For instance, he bought Britt a triple-banded Victorian engagement ring of emeralds, diamonds and rubies. Then came a sports car, a Dachshund dog, a diamond-studded brooch, a black mink coat and so on. Norman Hartnell, the Queen's couturier, was hired to design her wedding dress and they were married on 19 February 1964.

*At Peter and
Britt's wedding
reception. Bottom
left is Peg*

Opposite: *Peter photographs Britt during the making of* The Bobo, *1967*

When we were staying in Rome during the early 60s, the paparazzi thing was just beginning. The photographers were trying to conjure shots of Britt and Peter Sellers together from up trees through ludicrous lenses. Now, as we know post-Princess Diana, it was not only ridiculous, but exceedingly dangerous.

My father was good with the media. He always had a smile for them, even if sometimes he did resent their intrusions. But he was someone who liked being famous. In the early 70s, when his career was in a lull, although he claimed he didn't need the fame and the attention, you could sense he dearly wished he still had it. It is a bit of a let down to go from adulation to rejection.

Work took my father to the States. He managed to get Britt to quit her film *Guns at Batasi* (1964) at a personal cost, to him, of sixty-two thousand dollars. It was Easter, and Sarah and I were summoned to California, which was fine as we were to do a trip around Disneyland. For the visit to Disneyland, my father, in his

Sarah, Britt and Michael

usual flamboyant way, organized a helicopter to deliver us. Shortly
after the trip, and while only in his late thirties, he was to be hit by
a series of heart attacks that nearly killed him.

We had spent Saturday at Disneyland, and I, for one, wasn't
keen to leave. My father gave in to our pleading and said we could
stay longer, and so went and booked rooms at a local hotel. On the
following day, Sunday 5 April, we all drove slowly back to Beverly
Hills. We sang to the radio commercials in the car and made up
bizarre lyrics. We, the children, went to bed quite early and my
father and Britt had dinner alone.

He was looking tired at this time, and under a fair bit of
pressure, particularly from 20th Century Fox who had confronted
him with a 1.5 million dollar breach of contract suit over Britt's
walking out on *Guns at Batasi.*

That evening, walking across his bathroom floor, he suddenly
stopped as he experienced what appeared to be a sudden attack of
severe indigestion. He told Britt that his chest felt like it was on
fire. The 'fire' got worse. Dr Rex Kennamer was called. My father
was informed that he had had a mild heart attack. But his
condition worsened during the following twenty-four hours. He
had several further attacks, and for a time it was very touch and go.

But he made a remarkable recovery – and against all odds.

During the exercise era, as I call it, we both got pretty fit as I
was into cycling, and this became an appealing way for him to take
exercise. We would do as much as twenty miles a day. The other

*A pose for
Christmas 1967.
Peter is in
costume as the
Bobo. On the wall
is a photograph of
baby Victoria*

part of the fitness campaign was the trampoline he kept in the back yard at Elstead, where he returned to recover.

This was a good phase in both our lives, because we bonded in a way that only ever happened again right at the final moments of his life. We would stop in country lanes and just soak up the views of the English countryside; of fields and church spires. We would also tell each other jokes, and on one occasion – somewhat too late – he gave me my 'birds and bees' talk. He gave a stilted lecture, which I recall as being fairly awkward for both of us.

After a bike ride, we would go back home to watch a movie or, more often than not, play Scalextric. Then he would get the car out – usually one of his Ferraris – and we'd tinker about with it for a while before going out for a drive. Life was very good at this point – almost idyllic. The compulsory need to recuperate had made him very fatherly. There were no flare-ups or tantrums. It is a shame it didn't last, but I presume that as his health improved, his appetite to throw himself back into his 'real' world developed. In a year or so, his life, and therefore our lives in relation to his, were back to where they used to be.

The fitness and health kick which should have become a permanent feature of his life, started to wear thin after a time. As Spike always says, 'He wore slip-ons so he didn't have to bend down and tie his laces, he was that lazy.' So other than the brief period following his first heart attack, he didn't exercise, and the family-man image slowly eroded.

Outside Peter's house at Elstead

Britt looked after me during this period. When we walked down the street together, she would grab my arm to keep attention away from me. She was very aware of our position as Peter Sellers' children, and always remained very protective of us. It was the basis of our friendship and perhaps explains why it has continued right up to this day.

My father's marriage to Britt stumbled on for four years. A woman normally noted for her effervescence, Britt became down and dispirited. It was sad to see that the pressure of being married to such an unpredictable, unsettling man had taken its toll. She was granted a divorce in London on 18 December 1968, on the grounds of mental cruelty. She was also awarded care and control of Victoria – their daughter from the union – with joint custody.

Prior to Britt's return to Sweden, where she intended spending Christmas, she stayed at the Dorchester. My father offered her his flat in Clarges Street to use as a temporary base. With Victoria in tow it seemed to make sense, so she accepted his offer.

That evening, she joined him for dinner in a party which included the likes of Julie Christie, Warren Beatty, Roman Polanski and the tragic Sharon Tate. (Sharon Tate was horrifically murdered the following year by the notorious Charles Manson.) By the end of the evening, he was apparently feeling melancholy. When Victoria had gone to bed, he took out a double-barrelled shotgun and pointed it at Britt, his finger on the trigger. He told her he was going to kill her.

Britt somehow managed to keep calm and pacify him by saying that if he did he would spend the rest of his life in prison, and that that would destroy him and so on. Eventually, she was able to take the gun away from his trembling hands. But we didn't see Britt for a long time after that.

My father's next marriage soon followed. Miranda Quarry fitted the pattern he was starting to establish – good-looking, blonde, impressionable, circa twenty-one years of age and fairly naïve. The one thing that I recognized, even though I was only about fifteen, was his inability to handle a relationship with anyone of a mature, experienced age and nature – like my own mother. He wouldn't have been able to deal with the challenges of a grown-up relationship.

Miranda was a debutante whose place in society was enhanced by the fact that her stepfather was Lord Mancroft, the former Conservative cabinet minister and Chairman of Cunard.

Peter with his third wife, Miranda Quarry

The summer following the start of their romance, we sailed to Cap Ferrat to visit David Niven and his wife, Hjordis. We then took time out in Monte Carlo. Miranda didn't like the boat very much. She would have been happier staying at waterfront hotels.

Any shared happiness that had originally inspired their marriage didn't last too long. Always uncertain about marriage, my father kept his relationship with Miranda in limbo for about two years, subjecting her to the usual bout of tantrums, suspicions and general qualms. He always had a detailed explanation for his marriages and their failures, but when ever asked why he married Miranda, he could only reply, 'I really don't know!' It is quite feasible that loneliness at that time had much to do with it. He wasn't good at being by himself, he would brood away the hours in his own company. He certainly always claimed that Miranda had called the shots forcing him into the situation, but just before the marriage to Miranda had taken place, he had rung both my mother and Britt to blame *them* for his predicament. It was a marriage doomed before it had even been consecrated. After a legal separation, she gained her freedom and soon after married Lord Nuttall.

Even before the marriage was over, my father had begun an affair with Titti – more formally addressed as Countess Christina Wachtmeister. Much subterfuge went on culminating in me having to pretend she was *my* girlfliend during the holiday I spent in Mexico with my father and Titti. The reason for this plot was that

Miranda's sister, Victoria, turned out to be visiting Acapulco at the same time. The subterfuge didn't exactly work, Victoria one evening saying to me, 'Titti is with your father, isn't she? Don't worry, the secret is safe with me. I shan't rush home and tell Miranda.' To be honest, I was so fed up with the game by now, I doubt I'd have cared much if she'd chosen to announce it on prime-time television!

A further memory of that time is when we returned home and my father tried to pair me off with Titti's elder sister. My potential girlfriend would have been older than my father's girlfriend! I wasn't keen on that idea – as I didn't care for the notion of two sisters comparing notes. It could all have become a bit sordid.

The day after his divorce from Miranda Quarry, my father excitedly proposed to Titti. She wouldn't give a definite answer. Always unable to deal with rejection, he then got his secretary, Sue Evans, to telephone Titti to try and persuade her. Still no commitment was forthcoming. 'Doesn't she love me?' he asked.

As part of his method to win Titti, he entertained her on a lavish scale. If it wasn't a private box at Royal Ascot, it was dinner in the company of Cary Grant.

Cary complimented my father on his choice, and wished him every success, which seemed to accelerate his desire to marry her. In the process, he became over-possessive, as he was apt to do. He wanted to see her every day, and when this wasn't possible, he demanded a full explanation of her every movement.

*With Titti during
the making of* The
Return of the Pink
Panther, *1975*

Overall, though, their relationship was in good shape – better
than many of his previous ones under the type of pressure he could
apply – until, that is, Titti one day asked him to reimburse her for
the money she'd used in buying film for her camera. He was utterly
flummoxed.

'Why can't you pay for it yourself?' he asked her. 'I've paid for
your flight, and your hotel. What more do you want? Can't you
afford a few rolls of film?'

If Titti had asked for a Rolls Royce or any outlandish luxury,
he would without doubt have said, fine. But the thought of

rummaging around his pockets for a couple of dollars to pay for film was somehow a personal insult.

'Is this all I mean to you? Is this the price of your love?'

Considering how limited the funds of his childhood had been, my father still never considered himself a rich man. In fact, he would complain that he had four million pounds' worth of assets tied up in stock and property by his lawyers and accountants, which he was unable to access. He needed, he once told me, 'some spending money.'

Titti also asked him to compensate her for loss of earnings as a fashion model – this career having gone on hold during her time with him. Surprisingly, despite all of this, the relationship repaired itself, and he continued to be very affectionate with her once the initial shock and outburst were out the way.

I chatted with Titti on a flight from California to New York, and it was clear she was trying to know how to understand and deal with my father. 'One day, he is so wonderul,' she said, 'and the next, he sulks for no reason.' Finally, she said, 'How can I begin to understand him?'

I laughed and replied, 'It would be impossible to begin to answer that question. It would need a seminar to attempt to explain Dad's foibles.'

Once in New York, Titti and my father continued to jog happily along together. Indeed, he even told me on the quiet, 'Mike, I know Titti is one hundred per cent right for me.' I raised

various doubts. 'But I've known Titti nearly two years, now,' he
pointed out. 'How can it be wrong?'

He then showed me some nude shots of Titti he had taken.
'Now can you see why I want to marry her, Mike? Isn't she
beautiful?'

I wasn't going to argue.

Then their relationship plummeted into an abyss. They were in
Cyprus eating at a taverna, when a Cypriot began giving Titti the
eye at her table, and she responded. My father stormed off. He
grabbed his coat and chucked Titti's at her, smashing bottles, glasses
and crockery – much to the entertainment of those gathered.

Then came the Swiss preview for *The Return of the Pink
Panther* (1975). Titti chose not to go, so he took her sister, Anna,
and a friend, this being one of the most important occasions in his
life. So much was at stake with this new Panther film and, being its
star, he was naturally carrying the full weight of the project. At this
moment in time, no one was sure if the public still loved or even

wanted more Clouseau. There had been a long gap – over ten years – between this one and the previous two. The rest, as they say, is history: the film was one of his biggest ever. Feeling euphoric, he was keen to make amends with Titti. He actually forgot to say goodbye to me at Heathrow as he darted off in search of her.

It was a lost cause. Titti had abandoned all hope that they were in any way suitable for reconciliation. Another chapter in the romances of his life was closed for good.

Peter and Liza Minnelli in London, 1973

In 1973 there was the much publicized affair between my father and Liza Minnelli. The all-singing all-dancing 'Liza with a zee' would have made an interesting stepmother.

His courtship of Liza was a very public affair, and they would be photographed holding hands and kissing and behaving like a young couple with a big crush on each other. Which is possibly all their relationship amounted to.

During the third week of this, I began to sense all was not as it should have been in their Garden of Eden. My father began complaining that he never saw her on her own. She was always surrounded by an entourage.

'How do we get rid of these people when we marry?' he asked her.

'Get rid of them!' came Liza's shocked response. 'These are my friends, Peter. They're always gonna be my friends.'

And that was the beginning of the end of that particular romance.

There was a time when all of us in the family thought my father was going to marry Mia Farrow. One afternoon, he took me with him to visit his tailor. Afterwards, he said, 'Come on. We're going to Frank Sinatra's flat in Grosvenor Square.'

Fair enough. We rang the bell and the door was answered by a nervy, fair-haired waif, who was, of course, Mia Farrow. This little visit prompted a second meeting. Mia visited Brookfield and fell in love with the place. Sarah and I showed her around the grounds.

Thinking back, she is one of the few women in his life to have remained no more that just a friend – no strings attached. Maybe he knew about Sinatra's interest in Mia, and decided he didn't want to run the risk of wearing concrete socks! Whatever, once she'd returned to the States, her name didn't come up again.

The most famous woman in his life, and one who was to remain an unstinting friend throughout, was undoubtedly HRH Princess Margaret.

The first time I met Lord Snowdon and Princess Margaret was at a party at our Elstead home. In anticipation of their visit, my father gave me a lesson in how to bow and, likewise, Britt showed Sarah how to curtsey.

The royal couple would often visit us. We had a cinema, which was a twenty-seater arrangement. The most popular movie was a burlesque involving Princess Margaret impersonating Peter Sellers impersonating Princess Margaret. My father also did a skit on a one-legged golfer, and Britt played a movie queen.

One day, we all went to Windsor to water-ski on the lake. We had lunch and paddled around. All very informal. I can't say normal, because it isn't normal to live at Windsor, have your own park, own lake and so forth. I remember Princess Margaret always having a need for cigarettes. I can even recall her saying, as if I'm likely to forget, 'Where are my bloody fags!'

One summer, Sarah, me, my father and Britt, went on his boat to the Aga Khan's outpost in Sardinia. Sarah, who had never heard of the Aga Khan, asked, 'Who is the Earl of Cannes?'

Princess Margaret and Snowdon were guests of the Aga Khan on *his* yacht. The boats drew up to each other, we all said our hellos, and I started climbing around the yacht. Then a voice said, 'Hi Mike, how are you?' and I turned round to see Princess Margaret sunbathing up on the top deck.

On one occasion, I accompanied my father and Lord Snowdon to the coast to try out a new boat Tony had bought. We trailered it down behind a jeep. My father and Tony were up front, and the rest of us were in the back. Along the way, we picked up some hitchhikers who had no idea who the driver and passenger were.

Peter with Princess Margaret. Behind the public formality was a private friendship

At the end of the day, Princess Margaret and Peter Sellers were kindred spirits: that's what drew them together. Whatever their relationship began as, they went on to maintain a long-lasting friendship throughout his turbulent life. Their relationship definitely worked better one to one. Once among people, she was naturally compelled to take on the mantle of her station.

My father's fourth and final bride was a budding young actress called Lynne Frederick. His pursuit of her and eventual marriage to her were, from our family's point of view, the beginning of a catastrophe. She came to hold great power over him, and it is more than likely that his decision to change his will – to leave us nothing; not even a memento of our family history – to make her sole recipient of everything was, indeed, *her* decision. It is something that has taken the Sellers family a long time to come to terms with, and many of my memories of Lynne are not particularly happy ones. Whatever short-term benefit she had, it didn't bring her happiness or success as an actress. She was dead by the age of forty-one from alcohol and drug abuse.

Though slightly darker haired than his previous wives, Lynne was young and attractive and therefore fitted the bill. What concerned me most at the start of their relationship was not only did we have yet another step-mother on the horizon, but this time it was one younger than me! My father wanted to look young for his bride so he decided to have his puffy eye bags

*Peter with his
fourth wife, Lynne
Frederick*

removed by cosmetic surgery. And in the same way, he dealt with
his double chin.

After they married in Paris on 18 February 1977, Lynne made it
clear she was keen to have children. My father wasn't quite so keen,
and side-stepped the issue by presenting her with a Yorkshire terrier!

By the time Lynne came on the scene, the most pressing issue
was my father's declining health. He had long put off open-heart
surgery which terrified him. Instead he pursued more alternative
routes such as a visit to a group of 'psychic surgeons' from the
Philippines, who turned out to be charlatans.

Accepting he had been duped by the so-called 'psychic

surgeons', he thankfully returned to taking his heart pills and, with a pacemaker installed, he seemed, for a time, a much more content figure. Unfortunately, the pacemaker actually disguised the exact condition of his heart; something that would only emerge with his death.

One thing became evident with Lynne's arrival on the scene – key people in my father's life were now being replaced. Even the long-serving, ever faithful Bert Mortimer was ousted. Around this time, I took my then girlfriend and future wife, Kathy, to visit my father and Lynne in St Tropez. He was overseeing the building of his new house in Port Grimau. His marriage to Lynne still appeared to be a happy one, not least because she deferred to him in a way he hadn't experienced from the other women in his life, and there were moments when he reverted to his old self. He became ruffled one night when driving Lynne's new car, and gave high-speed chase to a Frenchman along a coastal road. 'Peter, don't drive like this,' Lynne screamed. 'This is *my* car and it's not run in, yet. What are you doing?'

'Damn your car!' he shouted. 'That Froggie needs carving up.' It was all very amusing. After about three miles of this, the Frenchman abandoned his vehicle and disappeared into a block of flats. My father, not one to give up easily, didn't leave it at that. He got out of the car and began screaming insults and hooting the horn.

Suddenly I was twenty-six and married. My father had come to the wedding and it had been wonderful. Kathy and I had lived together for five years prior to marrying yet, six weeks later, she had left me high and dry for someone else. My father got to hear about this and a couple of months later rang me up at my flat. I wasn't doing much at the time other than staring out of windows feeling fairly sorry for myself. He said, quite simply, 'What are you doing?'

'Nothing.'

'I've heard about the marriage. Do you want me to send over some people to sort out the fella?' He often came out with these sort of unexpected suggestions, which he saw as practical solutions.

I said, 'It's all right, Dad, I don't really want her back,' which was true now that the dust had begun to settle.

He hated any form of public transport. He would do Nazi salutes at Customs officials, and then he'd walk straight through. They would say, 'We do know who he is … but we could actually arrest him for that, you know.'

'Well, I'm off to Switzerland. Do you want to come?'

'Yes. When does the plane leave?'

'When we get there,' he said. 'It's up at Stansted and when we arrive, we take off for Switzerland. It's a private plane.'

Well, that all sounded cool to me.

He hated any form of public transport, and unless he flew privately, he could be quite exacting, to say the least. For instance, he would do Nazi salutes at the Customs officials, and then he'd walk straight through. They would say, 'We do know who he is and we will look through his luggage if we want to, but we could actually arrest him for that, you know.' What could I say? What could *anyone* say?

The private jets gave him total privacy. They have their own Customs post to wave you through, and with the only luggage being your own, they virtually wheel it out to the aircraft immediately. You don't even have to go through the main terminal.

It transpired after he had died, that in the last eighteen months of his life he spent 750,000 dollars on private jet travel! And that was in 1980: he would have been better off going out and buying his own plane.

I recall how struck I was by how short the stewardess was on board the flight from Stansted – until I realized how difficult it is to stand in a small private jet. She was about four foot eight and could wander up and down without having to bend double.

His invitation to travel with him had taken place at eleven in

Opposite:

On my wedding

day

the morning. By four that afternoon we'd taken his private jet to Geneva, taken the small air-taxi up to his Gstaad chalet, and were sipping tea together in the Swiss Alps.

Alone in Switzerland, other than the presence of his assistant, we were able to talk. Lynne was in America, so we could be ourselves, and we really got on extremely well.

His health had visibly deteriorated. He had become very gaunt and was living on a bizarre diet of various heart pills and pills for diabetes – an illness he'd developed by this time (and that I would develop, myself, some years later).

It had become standard procedure to call his bathroom cabinet Boots The Chemist. Any drug you needed was probably in there. Many of his health problems possibly originated from the various drugs he'd taken down the years. He took Amyl Nitrate – a drug he'd first got into after marrying Britt, it being linked to better sex. And there was loads of other stuff that was available to him in the early 60s.

Once settled at his chalet, he tried to open conversations on the previous failings of our relationship, but I wasn't ready to go into all that yet, so held him back. With hindsight I obviously regret that, because I felt we were gradually building towards discussing things of a deeper and darker level, which would have hopefully cleared a path for the future.

I felt we were making a beginning as two adults who happened to be father and son *but I wasn't ready for it*. He was equipping himself to accept me as a grown-up man, and that path had been eased, in a way, by my briefly experiencing the sort of mess he had endured on many occasions in his nightmare world of marriage. In other words, I think my problem gave us the basis for discussion purely and simply because he could relate to divorce and matrimonial problems having been there so often. Certainly, he found it easier to contend with than the unpredictability of an irreverent child; the teenage years; the problems of leaving home to reside at boarding school; the disruptive behaviour and so on.

Though practical with electronics, stereos and general gadgetry, he was not practical around the house. While I was at Gstaad, he called someone out to fix his gate. 'I could have done that for you in five minutes, Dad,' I told him. Apart from anything, it would have saved money. But by that time in his life, he simply paid for everything. The fact that you may have to pay through the nose had become meaningless to him. You paid money, and you got what you wanted. With the sort of wealth he had, I'm sure he lost sight of the real world. I know he never fully comprehended that I didn't have the cash *he* had. For instance, he never understood why I didn't chase the sort of women *he* chased. On one occasion, I tried to explain to him. 'I can't afford to entertain a woman like that, Dad. I can't even afford to go out and buy her a trinket, let alone take her to dinner somewhere exclusive. Not on a carpenter's wages!'

'Well, you've got a rubbish job,' he said.

'At least it's a job.' But he didn't really understand my point.

For the most part, Switzerland was a levelling time when we could come at problems as adults, but we would part company still needing further talk and work on what we had both initiated.

After all, my father was a very difficult man to be with. You had to be whatever he wanted you to be at the time. He didn't make any allowances for you; *you* had to make allowances for him. If you didn't, then you were instant history.

I recall being knackered by the time we'd had dinner on that first night in his Swiss chalet. I probably hadn't been sleeping that well due to circumstances at home. My father said to his assistant, 'What's the matter with him? Why is he so quiet?' He tried to explain to my father that I might be very tired – that it had been a long day. Because *he* wasn't tired, he couldn't take the information on board.

'What do you think of the house?' he asked me some time after we'd arrived.

'It's the first place you've had that feels a little bit permanent and could possibly be a home,' I told him, and it was true. He was based there for tax reasons, but this could certainly have become his one true home as he grew older and his health deteriorated. I can't claim he was more relaxed there than anywhere else, because he was not someone who was ever relaxed. I added, 'And maybe I can have a room in this house I can call my own?' I'd not had that since Elstead: all his other various addresses had been temporary.

You just bunked down where there was a spare spot. I felt we could be a family there. He really liked the idea of that. He started on about doing this and doing that, but at that time all I could say was, 'No, Dad, I have to get back to London to work. I have a house there and I have to pay for it.'

'That's not a problem, Mike,' he began.

'No, *I've* got to pay for it, Dad.' After a while, he accepted the trials and tribulations of a normal mortal's life and stopped badgering me into staying on indefinitely.

We went out for a spin in his Porsche. Do you like it?'

'Yes, I do.'

'Do you want one?'

'Yes, I want one desperately,' I replied – and he knew I did, because we were both car fanatics – 'but not till I can afford to buy one.'

The one single thing making him happy at this time was that United Artists agreed to pay him one million pounds to return as Clouseau. Paradoxically, they had paid Blake Edwards the same figure *not* to direct a new Panther, knowing very well that Sellers and Edwards had vowed never to collaborate again on a picture – a little sad considering the great work they had done together and the equally great friendship that for years they had shared.

Other than that incentive, every day life was if anything bleaker than before. He no longer socialized, not being physically up for it, so saw few people while Lynne was away. And he

Peter and his Porsche

fumbled with everything he touched – this man of gadgets suddenly could no longer even recall how to switch on the video machine. And he was full of sentimental recollection. It was as if the past was everything and the present and future nothing – which, in truth, is exactly how it had become.

He even began talking about my mother, Anne. He described her as being the best of his four wives – which is probably why he never fully let go – and that he regretted his infatuation with Sophia Loren, which had been the chief cause of his marriage to my mother falling apart. 'Otherwise, Mike, we might still have all been together as a family,' he sighed. Then he added, 'What do you think of that Sophia Loren? She didn't even mention me in her book!'

That made me chuckle, because only a few days earlier he'd been complaining about Britt's book and how she had used his name to promote sales.

His appearance by this time was frightening. His face was hollow – almost emaciated. When he took time to study himself in the mirror, he would make positive sounds about a heart operation, but I think we both knew – though it was never expressed – that the time for all that had passed. It wasn't a question of if he was going to die, but of when.

And yet, he was only fifty-four. That sounds so young, only nine years older than I am at the time of writing.

He made the decision that he would seek medical help and go through with an operation. He called Dr Sugarman in Los

Opposite:

Peter, in costume for The Magician *of Lublin, is visited by Sophia Loren*

Angeles, the man who had steered him through his first heart problems in 1964.

My father knew it was going to be a gamble; his health was hardly up to traumatic surgery, but I saw it as a bigger gamble than I think he did. If he walked more than a matter of yards, he would have to pause for breath. Even climbing a few stairs would leave him puffing. This wasn't the best condition to take on a major operation.

That was in February 1980. We parted on good terms and I made a further visit to his Gstaad chalet in June of that same year, when he was writing the new *Pink Panther* movie – the one with*out* the producer, director and writer Blake Edwards.

We discussed plans to have Christmas out there. It would have been a serious step towards establishing family life with him after so many wilderness years.

As a young man, I'd always wanted my father to come out with me to the pub for a pint of beer, or, to come and watch a cricket match with me. There was even a transport café I knew, where the food was superb, and I would have loved to have taken him there – to a real environment. He had always relied on safe, smart restaurants for fear of being recognized and having to live up to expectations that no mortal could have really lived up to; for it's a definite thing with comedians that they always feel they have to perform – that they have to be funny.

He said to me at this time, 'Mike, I would have loved to have gone out with you like that when you were a boy, but don't you understand why I couldn't?'

It was to me a further sign of improved communication that we could talk like this. But fate can be very cruel. Before that summer was fully underway, my father was dead.

Years earlier, my father had seen a clairvoyant, who told him he would live until the age of seventy-five. He seriously believed this. He had been told he would be wealthy and successful and experience a major illness in the middle of his life. It seemed almost logical, therefore, that the final prediction would also come true. Like him, a part of me certainly believed – or perhaps just hoped – it would.

Strangely enough, I felt that when the final heart attack came, he didn't fight to live. It was one time too many. He gave up to it – accepted it. He didn't want to come back. At the age of fifty-four, he was looking at another twenty years of repetition. He had done it all. On top of that, he was a vulnerable person, never fully sure that the work he had done was of any great value. What could he do next? I also believe that when he peered in the mirror during those final months, he came to dislike what he saw. Not just physically, though he was in physical decline, but what he was like as a human being.

One of my father's prime motivators had been his fear of being ordinary – just another face in the crowd. Fame was his way out. He wanted to be noticed, and at the same time to enjoy the trappings of wealth: the expensive cars, toys, houses, women, and boats.

I think it is easy to fall into the trap of over-analysing Peter Sellers. Perhaps I'm guilty of it myself. The closest you will come to finding the 'real' Peter Sellers is to look at the character of Chance in his film *Being There* (1979). The comparison is irresistible. To look further than that is a wasted exercise. Trying to read much more into Peter Sellers than there actually was has become many a biographer's pastime. He was far more straightforward than people are willing to accept.

Had Peter Sellers lived, it would have been interesting to see what direction his life would have taken. He was talking about stopping acting and turning to directing, which is not an unusual move for an accomplished performer. He was only getting older, so directing would have made sense, as his physical condition would not have been such a major issue when behind the camera.

He passed away at 12.28 a.m. 24 July 1980. My last words to him were, 'See you tomorrow, Chinese Dentist.' (Tooth hurty!)

Can I sum up his life? Peter Sellers, star of stage, screen and labour exchange! His work speaks for itself. You turn on the TV, there he is and you remember *Clouseau: 'Is that your minky?'*

I'll leave the last words to the proverb used as a promotional slogan for his favourite film, *Being There*. They are somehow also fitting for my father, the man.

Life is a state of mind.

Opposite:

Peter enjoys being surrounded by pretty girls, after judging a beauty contest

FAMILY, FRIENDS

2

& COLLEAGUES

Anne Levy

The following recollections are from Michael's mother,
Anne Levy, who was the first wife of Peter Sellers.

t was several lifetimes ago when I first met Peter. I was a student at RADA, and he was a well-known variety artist and radio performer. His agent Dennis Selinger, who was a good friend of mine, took me to see him in a radio show called *Ray's a Laugh,* in which Peter played several characters. I was very impressed by his performance. Afterwards, the three of us went out to dinner and during the evening Peter invited me to see him do his stage act the following night. I went along and he was magical. I fell in love!

We continued to see each other regularly. We shared the same sense of humour and had a great time together. I had never met anyone quite like him. Then he took me to meet his mother, Peg. Well, this wasn't just a mother – this was an ogre! She not only dominated Peter, but also his poor father, Bill, who was a kind, gentle man who never got a word in edgeways – Peg said it all!

Peter was an only child and a showbusiness child. He toured with his parents from the time he was born. Bill was a musician, and Peg did a posing act in front of a magic lantern in her mother's touring show. However, Peg and Bill split up when Peter was still very young, and so there was little male influence in his life. There was only his possessive mother, who didn't believe in discipline and who thoroughly spoiled and smothered her son. Peter said he never knew exactly what happened, but a long time later his mother took him in a car up to Leicester Square in London's West End, and there was his father standing on a pavement. They picked him up and took him home. Once again Bill was back in his life.

Peg resented me on sight. In fact, she telephoned my mother (a complete stranger to her) and said, 'I don't want your daughter to have anything to do with my son – she will ruin his life!' My mother was shocked and didn't want me to see Peter. Nevertheless, we became engaged and married about fifteen months later. My parents came to the wedding, but Peg refused to have anything to do with it.

One day soon after the marriage Peg rang up and I answered the phone. During the conversation she said to me, 'Peter doesn't have to think for himself, I do it for him.' I told her to 'go to hell!' and slammed the phone down. She did not speak to me for about two years, but tried every way she could to split us up. She even invited old girlfriends of Peter's to meet him up at her flat. She knew that he was sentimental and dwelt on the past and thought that this might be a way of getting rid of me.

Peg never really let Peter go, and right up to the end of our marriage, she would ring him every single day. If there was a fog outside, she'd tell him to be careful, and if it was cold, she'd tell him to wrap up warmly.

Christmas time in the Sellers' household was always a bizarre event. We would ask my parents for lunch and have the full works – the meal, the crackers, the presents; then they would leave at about four p.m. Then about an hour later Peg and Bill would arrive and we would repeat the entire festivities. We celebrated Christmas twice in one day, our two families never actually meeting.

Over the years, Peg came to accept me and, in fact, when Peter and I decided to part, she begged me not to leave him. When I remarried, she would say to her driver (who also used to drive me) 'Where does that darling girl live? Take me to her flat.' She would then sit outside my home without saying a word. The poor woman died an alcoholic.

After the war, Peter began his professional career at the Windmill Theatre, which of course was famous for its nude shows. He did an act that combined drumming and doing impressions. I can't begin to imagine what that was all about. He said his real problem was when he came off stage and was surrounded by chattering naked women.

He was a good drummer, a brilliant impressionist and a great raconteur, but his real ambition was always to become a straight actor.

One summer, Peter was doing a variety show at the end of the pier, Southsea, and after several weeks he became dissatisfied. He hated repetition. When I went into his dressing-room one evening, he was wearing a long black coat and a large Fagin-type hat. 'What are you doing?' I said. He replied, 'I can't stand it any more. I reckon if I go on stage in this coat and hat, I won't be able to see the audience and, with a bit of luck, they won't be able to see me!'

On another occasion, while working in Coventry in a long-running production with Spike (Milligan) and Harry (Secombe) he got so fed up one night that he said, 'This audience just don't get it – they're raving idiots, I think I'll put on a record.' Sure enough that is exactly what he did. Instead of his act, he just played records!

Peter continued to find repetition difficult even when he made the transition from impressionist to actor and was starring in a play called *Brouhaha,* which was directed by Peter Hall. I was sitting in the audience one night when half-way through a scene, Peter walked down to the front of the stage, suddenly stopped, looked very shocked, and said, 'Christ! I've just walked into the fourth wall!' Then he continued with the text. On another occasion, he was dancing around the stage with a girl and got so carried away that they actually fell off the stage into the orchestra pit. He landed on his back with the girl on top of him, and all that could be heard was Peter saying, 'What the fuck are we doing down here!'

I think directors had to give up on him in the end. Peter Hall once said in an interview that he would just let Peter do his own

thing. When Peter first started in a show, he would stick rigidly to the script but later he would go off at a tangent and improvise. His improvisations were always very funny but, I imagine, very unnerving for his fellow actors.

Peter was always extremely inconsistent – always looking for something new. This applied not only to his professional life, but also to his private life. He loved new toys, new cars, new characters – new wives, too. But the fascination soon wore off. He was like a child. He never really grew up, and it made him very difficult to live with.

When we were first engaged, I spent half my time sitting outside garages while Peter looked at cars. That was a lifelong obsession with him. When I was three months pregnant for the first time, he went out and bought a large set of electric trains. It cost him about £400, which in those days was the price of a new car, and I made him take them back. I told him at least to wait and see if we had a boy. Needless to say, when Michael was born the trains came back. Peter was thrilled.

After the death of his parents, and despite our divorce, I remained the one constant in Peter's life. I'd known him long before he became internationally famous, and I was always around. He would ring me up all the time, even after I'd remarried. It would either be to talk to me about the children or to tell me about something funny that had happened to him. He would begin, 'I've got to tell you, Annie...'

Once he told me about the time he was invited to stay at Windsor Castle. He said he was absolutely overwhelmed, and when he was being taken to his room he thought, 'Hold on a minute – I'm Peter Sellers from 211B High Road, East Finchley – what the hell am I doing here?'

Peter also brought all his future wives to be 'vetted' by me. It was crazy. He even brought Liza Minelli over during the time he was going out with her. I remember Liza following me out to the kitchen and saying, 'He must be mad to have left you!' I just laughed. He didnt leave me. I left *him*. I do wish Peter had had a happy second marriage though, as I did.

When we were married, every character that Peter ever played came home with him and they merged with the real man. In *The Millionairess* his character became obsessed by the character played by Sophia Loren – and, of course, Peter became obsessed with Sophia. He really did fall for her during the film and it was a nightmare. He would phone her day and night and even told me he could feel her presence in our bedroom. I don't think he ever had a physical affair with her, I think it was probably all in his head – but it seemed real at the time.

Then there was the film *Never Let Go* in which he played a very unpleasant villain, and it was that nasty character who used to come home to me every night. So it went on – in each film I had a different husband!

Peter and I were together for about fifteen years, but finally I

Left: The Millionairess, *1960.*

Below: *Peter and Sophia, still friends in the 1960s*

*What do you think of **that** Sophia Loren? She didn't even mention me in her book!*

went through a period of actually hating him. Strangely enough, it was through him that I met my second husband, Ted Levy. Peter and I had a dreadful row and I went to stay with friends to get away from him. While I was away he sold our home in Chipperfield without telling me, and bought a flat in Hampstead. It was only a shell and Peter found a young South African architect to design it. I was furious and wanted nothing whatsoever to do with it but Peter begged me to meet the architect and take an interest in the flat. When finally I did, the architect was Ted, who would eventually change my whole life.

Peter and I moved into the flat but as far as I was concerned our marriage was over and I soon left him. I went to stay with my parents in Hertfordshire. Peter was devastated. He arrived on the doorstep uninvited one day and I let him come in. When he saw my parents, he said, 'Who are these old people?' I wasn't sure at the time if this was for real or if he was giving another performance, so I took him back in the car and drove him home. On the way back, he did not seem to know who I was or who *he* was – he appeared to have completely lost his memory.

I got him back to Hampstead, walked him up to his flat, but the minute we entered he slammed the door and locked it. 'Right. Now you're not leaving!' he said. 'If you try, I'll jump off the balcony and land on top of you.' I called our doctor, an old family friend, and he stayed with Peter while I left. It was very scary – he was a very convincing actor.

Peter was two people. There was Peter the actor, and Peter the person. The actor was self-assured and brilliant and I admired and respected him tremendously. The person, on the other hand, had incredibly low self-esteem and never knew how he should behave. In the end, I could not cope with him. It was Peter the person, who once came to a birthday party for our daughter, Sarah, at my home soon after I had remarried. He was at the pinnacle of his career, and between wives. Watching him looking wistfully on, I recall thinking, 'You are probably the saddest person I know.' He had everything he'd ever wanted professionally and financially, yet he had nothing – not even his children.

In the end, there was no resentment between us. As his great friend David Lodge once said, it didn't matter what he did, in the final analysis you still liked him. That is so true. I liked him, and so did Ted. We ended up as friends.

Peter was a strange and difficult man who never really knew who he was. He buried himself in the characters he played. I remember once seeing him staring at himself in the mirror, and after a long time he said, 'That's who I am – I'm just a big fat jolly boy!'

Opposite:

With Bill Cosby on

The Cosby Show

Victoria Sellers

Victoria Sellers, who lives in Los Angeles, is Peter Sellers'
daughter with Britt Ekland.

Opposite:

*Britt and Peter on
the set of* The
Bobo, *1967*

'Actor. Comic. Genius. Jet-setter. Influential performer whose
films and characters still inspire (e.g. Casino Royale as
forerunner or Austin Powers). Moody. Tortured. Lover. Father.
Husband.'

Peter Sellers has been described as all of the above. For me,
'Father' is the one that matters most. Yes, he was moody. And he
was a man who seldom let his real self be seen. He was perpetually
'on' – always in character.

He was not someone who necessarily fitted into the ideal
parent model, but then who does? My father was a man of larger-
than-life passions. And if we did not have the most stable of
relationships, with a great deal of time spent together, my
memories of the quality of time that we spent together have given a
special balance to my life.

My father's foibles are well chronicled. His beliefs and quirks
may seem 'out there' to some, but their positive influence still
lingers and affects the way I live today. I remember when I went to
visit him in London and his horrified reaction to my 'outrageous'
clothing. It was the colour that caused the concern. He was a
practising Buddhist, and purple was a colour with negative
associations in their doctrine. And, of course, my favourite colour

was purple! I still feel touched by his reaction – how special I felt when he bought a new wardrobe for me – and how much he cared about my spiritual well-being. Since then, I've never worn purple. And while that may seem strange to some, to me it just made him unique and sweet.

To the world at large, Peter Sellers will be remembered predominantly for his characters and films. I'm a fan, too, and have my own list of favourites: *I Love You, Alice B. Toklas,* – *The Party,* – *What's New, Pussycat?* – *The Bobo* and *Being There.*

As an aspiring performer, I wish he were here to see my successes and failures, to give me his criticism and support. Most of all, though, I am simply a daughter who misses her father.

(Extract courtesy of *Mean* Magazine)

Spike Milligan

British comedy institution, Spike Milligan, shared a close friendship with Peter for years. They met after the war then formed the Goons.

I first met Peter at the Hackney Empire. He'd gone there to see Harry Secombe with his shaving act and raspberries! I met Peter in the bar and I remember he seemed to be very concerned about how he was dressed. He wore a trilby hat and was wearing an expensive raincoat and he was holding his gloves in his hand. I think he thought of himself as quite a dandy. But he had a latent sense of humour lurking there and we seemed to get on.

I became a very close friend of his. He took a great liking to me. I was pretty homeless at the time; my mother and father had gone to Australia and I didn't have a home so I slept on the floor

The influential A Show Called Fred, *predecessor of* Monty Python. *Among the notables are Graham Stark (back left), Peter (back right), Kenneth Connor (front left) and Mario Fabrizi (front right)*

in his bedroom on a pumped-up mattress. We stayed with his mother, who doted on him. (In fact, he was covered in dote marks!) They seemed to kiss over-affectionately and, first thing in the morning, he had a whining voice. When he woke up he'd say, 'Peg! Peg!' 'What is it, darling?' 'Can I have some tea, please?' 'Yes, darling.' During the night there'd be a leak in the mattress, and I woke up flat on the floor!

We would go into the breakfast room and have scrambled eggs on toast. Then he would want to drive me round in his car, so I had to go with him. He drove all over the place, but nowhere particular. His father was a strange character; very quiet – just sat in a corner. His mother was the dominant one.

In the course of events, Peter introduced me to this girl, Anne, of whom he was very fond. She was the first of several blondes he fancied. We picked her up, and she wanted to go to her friend's to pick *her* up. This second girl was June and she would eventually become my wife. During the evening, I pretended I was a foreigner and I was called Jules! This went on all the evening.

Peter had a tape recorder – we liked to slow it down and record it and then play it back fast. We had a thing called a minstrel, and he would sing in a very high voice. Then there was a shot 'Bang!' and a cry of pain. We got off doing these funny voices, and I realized he was quite good at it.

Somehow I got to writing (and I'm not quite sure how I wrote the first *Goon Show* script) and we did this thing called *Crazy*

People, but the only people who laughed were the band because we were using this outlandish musician's humour. We recorded the show with the band laughing, and bit by bit the band used to bring their wives and relatives along, and they had the same sort of sense of humour. So our first audiences were basically the band's family!

I suppose I changed the British sense of humour completely. When I think of it, I don't know how I did it but I did, and writing those shows was a big achievement in my life.

I also worked with Peter on television in *A Show Called Fred.* They were very funny shows. I remember one scene which I thought was hysterical. It was where a couple of vicars turn up at the door and knock and someone says, 'Yes?' And one vicar says, 'We are Jehovah burglars! We are being persecuted by the police for our beliefs.' 'What are your beliefs?' 'We believe that you've got a lot of money here!'

I was very pleased for Peter when he made it big in films, and it didn't change him. But he did keep changing cars so frequently I used to call them metal waistcoats. He would change them about every four or five weeks. But of course he was earning big money.

The Running, Jumping, Standing Still Film was filled with my ideas. One had Peter on a hill reading music through a telescope, then he comes all the way down the hill to turn the page and goes back up again. The film won an award in San Francisco.

Peter called me up the middle of one night and told me to come over. I thought he was having trouble with one of his wives! I

The Goons mark St David's Day

in their own unique style

put a coat on over my pyjamas and drove over in my Mini. When I arrived, he gave me a piece of chalk and a torch and told me to climb into the boot of his Rolls Royce as there was a squeak. I got in the boot and Peter drove up and down the curb trying to make it squeak. Presently, I heard him pull up, a shuffle of feet and some voices. The boot opened and a policeman shone a torch in my face, recognized me and said, 'Oh, it's *you!*'

On another occasion, there was a knock at my door and it was Peter just wearing a hat and a pair of shoes. He asked, 'Do you know a good tailor?'

I always knew he would suffer with his heart. He was overweight and he bought shoes without laces so that he didn't have to bend down to tie them up. His illness frightened him a little bit; he started to go for long walks and bike rides, and things like that, but the damage had been done in his cholesterol days.

I went into the actual room when he was dying and I came outside and a reporter said, 'What do you think?' And I said, 'I think he'll make it.' That was about the worst prediction I've ever made in my life.

I miss him very much, I really do. I miss the comedy side. His pictures were funny but they were very straight, square comedy. Mind you, he did that French voice very well. But he said he was never happier than when doing the Goon shows.

David Lodge

The actor David Lodge knew Peter for thirty-five years, and is Michael Sellers' godfather. He worked in films with Peter on thirteen occasions.

I first met Peter early in 1945. I was in the RAF. I'd done five years in what I called the real Air Force, and there was in operation a show version of RAF entertainment called the Gang Show, run by Squadron Leader Ralph Reader. People like Dick Emery, Graham Stark, Cardew Robinson and Tony Hancock were in them. I applied and went to see Ralph Reader, and I was drafted into what was left of two different shows, which were then amalgamated.

I was put into a hut with some musicians. There was a trumpet player, a pianist, a tenor sax, etc., and comics. And there was this plump, fat-faced boy with very curly hair and a lot of it. He was nineteen and I was four years older, twenty-three. I had been in the forces a long while, and it made me a sort of veteran. This young chap was very much the kid.

It was cold and the huts had a stove at each end. There was this big Welsh guy, and he was picking on this fat boy. I wasn't tough, but I was a little streetwise, and I had this big piece of iron with which I was trying to knock out some of the ashes that had formed at the back of the stove. I thought, this can't go on. So I went up to the big Welshman and said, 'Leave him alone.' He turned round and said, 'It's nothing to do with you.' I told him, 'It

might not be, but I'm telling you to leave him alone.' Then I
turned to the boy and said, 'And you; if you can't do anything
about it' – and I gave him this large piece of iron – 'hit him with
that. And if you don't, *I* will.' Which was a stupid thing to say, but
it sorted the problem. And that was the beginning of a lifelong
friendship where I became a sort of big brother to the boy –
Peter Sellers.

When we were transferred to Dieppe, I first saw Peter's desire
to be someone else. His insecurity stemmed from the fact that he
wasn't happy with who he was: he was only happy when he pulled
on another character. We did a sketch where Peter played a Group
Captain but, strangely enough, we had another chap – Clifford
Henry – who did impressions. Peter's main thing was drumming.
He was a very good drummer.

One night he took the hat, the wings and medal ribbons from
the box (he added to the ones he had from Burma) and he made
himself up, putting on a plaited beard and a turban. Then he went
out. I didn't see him do this – all I saw was some men saluting a
Sikh officer and, as he went by, it suddenly registered.

Later, we were in Germany. We performed the show, and as
usual the band finished the set. Peter did the solo, and he was
good. He reached a crescendo where he threw the sticks up in the
air and pulled two others out, and this was a show-stopper. The
audience were enjoying it so much that the only way we could all
get off was for me to come on and make an announcement. Well,

the audience weren't having any of that and started giving me the bird. I caught them out by pretending to introduce another number with a 'One, two, a one two – got you!' They'd gone quiet and I quickly introduced the boys in the band.

After the show we went back to the Sergeants' Mess, which was a very smart place. I wasn't with Peter, I was with a WAAF, and all of a sudden I heard laughter. I looked round and I could see Peter. He was sitting at a table surrounded by Sergeants and the Station Warrant Officer, who is an extremely important person. Peter was wearing a big moustache, his hair was parted in the middle and he wore a Squadron Leader's bars. I excused myself from the girl and, as I approached him he looked up and said in a special voice, 'Oh hello! This is one of my lads. Lodge, come here.' I played along with it – I had to – and sat down mumbling, 'You stupid bastard! What are you doing?'

Up on a little platform, there were three or four terrible musicians who were trying to play jazz and couldn't do it. Peter said he could liven them up, and he did. He joined them on drums. Now, these officers had seen the earlier show, and you would think they would have realized it was the same fellow, even though we had all had a lot to drink. But they didn't. Peter came back and sat down, and I was worrying he was going to get into serious trouble. Then he started doing characters from ITMA, which was very big at the time, and his little audience of NCOs fell about laughing. I was stone-cold sober by now.

After a while I said, 'Sir, we have to go. We've got to get up very early in the morning.' Peter replied, 'Yes, I suppose so. Look. here, chaps, my man has just given me a reminder. It's time for us to push off. It's been a delight.'

We got up and the Station Warrant Officer marched with us to the door of the mess and thanked Peter and his men for the show, and said that if ever we were passing through again, we'd be made more than welcome, and he threw him a salute. Peter, who was actually the lowest rank possible in the RAF, calmly thanked him and we ran off.

At the end of service time you were demobbed. This was done on age and time given to the service. I was one of the senior boys so finished first. Peter came with me to catch the train, which was right on the Danish border. I always remember, we said our goodbyes as the train pulled in, and Peter stood there with tears in his eyes, like he was saying goodbye to his brother.

I didn't see Peter for a while after that but we both began making our way in show business. I was first to make it in films with *Cockleshell Heroes.* Meanwhile, he was in the Goons, and the boys celebrated with me. While filming, I nearly drowned. I was washed overboard, and my wet suit split in the arm and started to let in water and I couldn't make it to the surface. Two Royal Marines spotted my difficulties and saved me. It was all pretty frightening. Somehow the news got back to England and my father saw it in the Stop Press, and he got on the phone to Peter. He told

Peter where I was in Lisbon, and that night there was a call from
him. When I picked up the phone Bluebottle's (from the Goons)
voice came down the line: 'You rotten swine, you are not
drownded!' And that was Peter, and then he rang home and told
my father I was safe.

He used to call me from around the world. The telephone to
him was a toy. He called me once from the Seychelles just to tell
me it was too hot! Another time I was in Belgrade filming *The
Long Ships,* when I got a call from him in London. He was
between marriages and had hurt his ankle. It was in plaster, and
he'd stuck himself in the Dorchester hotel and was amusing
himself ringing all his mates round the world from the comfort of
his room.

I remember he rang from France and he knew Lyn, my wife,
was French. He spoke in a French accent saying what a prat De
Gaulle was. He'd had a bit to drink. Lyn was trying to tell him that
the French exchange was probably listening and he said, 'Well they
can kiss my royal French arse!'

He also rang from a yacht off Cannes where we had been
during 1945. This call was ship-to-shore, so whenever we finished
speaking we had to say 'over'. Along that coast there was an island
which was a nudist colony and Peter was standing with an
enormous pair of binoculars. What he was saying about these
people is unprintable! We had so many laughs. The first time I
ever saw a white telephone was at Peter's place in Finchley, which

is somehow typical that he should have been one of the first to own one.

Peter loved my parents so much that whenever he wrote from around the world he always put a PS to change the straw, because he had likened them to two little chicks in a nest. He used to tell me to look after them and that they had got to be clean! My mother was stricken with cancer which Peter found out about during a telephone conversation with me. He was due to go out with Princess Margaret and Tony that night but he held everything and told me to leave it to him. He arranged it all. The next day, she was in Harley Street with top people, and Peter picked up the tab. But it wasn't really a question of money. Peter wanted to help my mother. He gave her another fifteen months of life.

I made about thirteen films with Peter. One of the best was *Two Way Stretch,* and was a great film to do. It's very rare in films that you start shooting the first scenes first, but we did with this one. There was much giggling and ad-libbing. Things like Peter saying, 'Shut the window, there's a George Raft coming in.' Great fun.

Later came *Dock Brief* which basically had just four of us – Peter, Richard Attenborough, Beryl Reid and me. After the premiere, Lyn ordered all the Sunday papers because she thought I'd get good notices, and when they came through the door she took them away to read. Finally she called out to me that the *Observer* had given a terrible review, and right towards the end the

Opposite:

Peter as

Morganhall in

Dock Brief, *1962*

critic had written something like, 'For me the outstanding part in the whole miserable piece was the lodger brilliantly played by a Mr David Lodge, whom I strongly suspect was Mr Sellers in one of his many disguises.' The phone rang at nine o'clock and Peter came on saying, 'Sue the bastard!'

While still between marriages, Peter invited Lyn and me to the Dorchester for dinner with Billie Whitelaw, whom he'd recently directed in *Mister Topaze.* It was very pleasant and eventually Billie left, but Peter said to me, 'Don't go. Blake Edwards is on the next floor up.' I'd never met Blake, and he'd never heard of me. The American only knew a few British artists. Lyn and I were introduced, and Blake said something about hypnotizing Peter, which he proceeded to do. Peter did the business with the uncontrollable arm from *Dr Strangelove* and Lyn was looking at him with disbelief. When we left she said to him, 'Peter, you weren't really hypnotized?'

'No,' he smiled, 'but dear Blakey feels good if he thinks he has done it.' In other words, Peter gave a performance.

Peter told me how he formed the character for Chance, the gardener in *Being There.* Years before, he had had a gardener called Mr Dewberry: he was a lovely old boy. I remember him once saying something which tickled Peter. Mr Dewberry was pointing out various plants in the garden and saying, 'This one is temporary and this one is temporary and will die.' Then he pointed to another and said, 'But Mr Sellers, this one is *pernament*!' Peter loved that.

With Herbert Lom and Nadia Gray in Mister Topaze, *1961*

When Peter first went out to Hollywood, he used to go and have tea with one of his great heroes, Stan Laurel, who was living in a little flat. Peter told me that he had based Chance on old Mr Dewberry *and* Stan Laurel, and when I watch the performance, I can certainly see them both.

The last time I saw Peter was when he was making *The Fiendish Plot of Dr Fu Manchu.* He rang me from Paris, and it didn't sound as if he was getting along with the director. He told me he was going to re-shoot some scenes and that I was going to play a desk sergeant in a police station. I flew out to Paris and eventually Peter came down. I couldn't believe what I saw. He was always terribly affectionate with me, and he gave me a hug and kissed my cheeks; but his nose was pinched and he looked very, very ill. He died before the film was released, and they cut my scene out.

He did behave outrageously at times and I did chastise him, but at the end of the day I had great affection for him. Apart from being my buddy I owe him such a lot – he cared.

Opposite:

As Fu in his final film, The Fiendish Plot of Dr Fu Manchu, *1980*

Mr and Mrs Fred Kite on their wedding day. The photo on the mantelpiece in
I'm All Right, Jack, *1959*

June Whitfield

British comedy actress June Whitfield has worked with many of the great comedians, and is best known for her appearances as the mother in *Absolutely Fabulous*.

I worked with Peter on a song for a record which was recorded in Paris. It was about Sir Fred Kite and Margaret Thatcher, called *What About the Workers*. It wasn't used, as the story was he wrote to her to congratulate her on becoming Prime Minister and received such a charming letter back that he decided not to include the number – well, that was the story *I* heard!

Angela Morley

Angela Morley was the arranger and conductor of the orchestra on the Goon shows.

There was always a warm-up before the recording of the *Goon Show*, and it was pretty predictable. Peter would tell a joke about a violinist and it was very, very funny. It was about a band leader violinist doing society gigs and he would play the part with the accent and hold an imaginary violin with his hand right round the strings. Harry (Secombe) would tell a story then he would sing *Falling in Love with Love* and Peter would play the drums at the back. He would make a great play of playing a couple of notes and then going round to tune the drums. In the middle of this someone would fire a gun, which always used to make me jump! Peter did film the rehearsal once, and he had all the most expensive equipment. A copy must exist somewhere.

Peter was like a small boy; he loved all the things that boys like, from model aeroplanes to trains. I remember he liked Walkie Talkies, and he would be driving around in his car talking to his friends who all had Walkie Talkies, and he loved that.

It was interesting that if ever Peter couldn't be there for whatever reason, he did so many voices that they had to bring in about four people to replace him! He was such a remarkable comic actor, he gave so much to the show.

When I was doing the *Goon Show*, I learned to fly and I was taught by an ex-RAF pilot, who happened to be a great fan of the Goons. During the flying lessons, he would be Major Bloodnok throughout! Or on another occasion, he would be Eccles. I persuaded Peter to make a record using these voices and talking about this instructor. I forget exactly what he did, but it was very, very funny and I left it for this instructor. I don't know if he ever got it!

The boys used to scribble cartoons on the back of the Goon scripts and Peter used to draw how he thought Bluebottle looked. Once, when he was making *I'm All Right, Jack* where he played a Trades Union leader, he had drawn a caricature of how he thought this person should look and amazingly that's exactly how he looked in the film.

There was an Italian restaurant that Peter and Spike used to like to go to. Alan Clare would play at the piano, and sometimes Spike would bring his trumpet. One night, Peter and Spike had been having a good time and had been consuming quite a lot of alcohol, and they started making up a Russian-style song. It would be very sad and slow, then speed up before going slow again. That was the kick Peter was on that particular night!

Max Geldray

Dutch-born Max Geldray played jazz harmonica on the *Goon Show*. Before the war, in Paris, he knew and worked with Django Reinhardt, Maurice Chevalier and Duke Ellington. In 1956, Max worked with Peter and Spike Milligan in the seminal TV series *A Show Called Fred* and *Son of Fred*. He moved to America in 1961.

I first met Peter at the trial recording of the *Goon Show*. It was recorded several months before the first show (1951). Peter called me Ploogie, and when he wanted to sound endearing, he would call me Plooge!

Peter and I had jazz and music in general in common, but our real bond was the *Goon Show*. We got along very well and lived near each other. Peter had an uncle in real estate who found a new block of flats being built. Peter got himself one and asked me if I

The Goons looking

misleadingly angelic!

wanted one, too. So I had one. As often happened, Peter instigated the whole thing.

He was ten years younger than me, and did ask questions and for advice but, invariably, he would do as he wanted. I stopped telling him about new cars because he would say, '*We* have to have one,' – never, '*I* have to have one.'

There was a new Ford in the races, and I told him it had won and that I was going to get one. He thought that was great, so we both ordered one through a mutual friend, a lady supplier, who could get you any car you wanted. She would simply pick up the phone, say it was for a VIP and that it had to be delivered immediately. Although we both ordered at the same time, Peter was particularly insistent on the 'immediately' aspect of his purchase and so got his first.

Anne, Peter and I went to an Auto Show, and he started looking at the Bentleys. Anne and I could see him talking to the salesman, and it seemed he was signing papers. I said to Anne that it looked as if the Bentley was sagging in the middle – which of course, it wasn't. She went over to Peter and said, 'Max says it looks like the Bentley's sagging in the middle,' and, at once, Peter said, 'I won't have it!' and walked away.

He was influenced by his friends, but I could also be influenced by him. Many times he would say, 'You've got to have it' whatever *it* happened to be, and I would end up buying the thing.

He had to have any and every new gadget; particularly cameras

and cine cameras: indeed, he would regularly go to camera shops –
every day, if he could. One day, he came to pick me up in his car to
take me to one of these camera shops. I told him that I needed to
buy a new bulb for my camera, and so we set off, in different cars
as it happened because I needed to go on somewhere afterwards.

We met up in the shop and the salesman showed us a new,
little camera from Switzerland, which was better than the others
and more progressive. Peter said, 'You've got to have it, yours is
broken.' I reminded him that mine was not broken, it just needed a
new bulb, which I bought and then left.

Some hours later, I returned home to find Peter's car parked
outside. He and Anne were in the living room, and in the middle
of the floor was a packet. He pointed to it and when I opened it
up it was to find the new camera. When he had something in his
mind, you couldn't argue. He really was generous. If there was
something I wanted, all I had to do was say a word and he would
buy it. Eventually, I gave up mentioning a lot of things to avoid
this happening.

I had a vein removed from my leg. It was only a small
operation and I didn't tell anyone I was having it done. However, it
got into the papers that I was in hospital having an operation, and
that made it look worse than it was. When I got home, my kitchen
was filled with flowers and fruit from Harry (Secombe), which was
typical of him. Peter ran in asking, 'What's up? What operation
have you had?' I explained it was only a minor one but that it

meant I couldn't walk for the moment. He saw the flowers and
fruit and asked who'd sent them. When told, it was enough for
him to insist I get straight into his new car that he had outside.
'But I can't walk,' I told him. 'I'll carry you!' And he did. He lifted
me from the living room all the way into his car.

We went round to a shopping centre. He told me to wait in
the car and listen to the radio, and this I did – for a long time.
Eventually, he returned followed by a man laden with parcels.
Peter told me, 'They're for you.' When we got home, we undid
them and they made up a complete new sound system, turntable
and every extra you can think of. Though I had a system, this one
was definitely newer and better.

We did a lot of touring and variety together. Peter really didn't
like being on stage on his own. You would tell the stage manager
how long you were going to do and you had to keep to it. In order
to spend less time on his own, he would come in on my act for
three minutes, and three minutes in my act meant three minutes
less on his own doing *his* act.

When we were in Wolverhampton, in a beautiful but
dilapidated theatre, I was on stage when I noticed a figure out of
the corner of my eye. I carried on as it wasn't unusual for the
Goons and I was used to it. This figure was wearing a dark mac
down to his ankles, a huge hat over his ears and eyes and large
boots. He shuffled towards me and I pretended I didn't know
what was going on. I shouted to the stage manager, 'What's

happening?' The 'figure' shuffled up and I called out, 'Help me! What are you doing?' Peter asked, in one of his voices, 'What is this theatre?' (Peter was definitely a genius when it came to voices. After listening to you for five minutes, he would be able to do your voice. We would have a whole conversation like that. It was most extraordinary.) I told him we were in Wolverhampton and he looked around the place – the audience, of course, realizing it was him. He said, 'It could do with a good burn down!' and promptly walked off to applause.

The show came and went and as it was a Saturday, we drove home so that we could record the *Goon Show* the next day. Sometimes, if the venue was a long way off, we would have to drive all day Sunday to be there. Anyway, the next morning the telephone rang and it was Peter. 'Guess what?'

'What?'

'The theatre in Wolverhampton has burned down!'

Somebody must have heard him and thought, 'That's a good idea.' I don't think it ever was rebuilt.

We had a good friendship and I miss him very much. I was very fond of him, and we never had an argument in all the years that I knew him.

Denis Norden

Denis Norden has been writing since the 1940s, and is particularly well-known for his partnership with the late Frank Muir, and his presentation of the series *It'll Be Alright On The Night*.

We first met Peter when Frank (Muir) and I were writing for anything we could get written things into, including the Windmill Theatre, where Peter was working. The chief bond which drew us all together was a club, which was like a restaurant, called *Daddy Allen's* which gave credit! So you could lunch on tick but more importantly, you could take radio producers, who were all like Ziegfeld to us, and give them a lavish lunch of what then passed as steak – it was horse, I believe – with an egg on top. For luxury purposes, it was like having a private jet! There were Spike, Alfred Marks and Harry Secombe. It was there that we met this group; all demobbed people from the services; people like Michael Bentine, Benny Hill and Peter. We were all of an age, of a generation, and we'd shared a common experience.

When I was writing in the forces, I would go as far as I could in being funny about the officers without standing accused of inciting to mutiny: this was an element we all carried on into comedy after the war.

Peter was first heard in *Showtime* (1949). I didn't write his pieces, he did his own thing. During this very formative time of his life, Peter was an impressionist.

To those of us who worked with him then, he was *always* an impressionist.

Being a good impressionist is like being a cartoonist or caricaturist; he points out certain salient features of somebody which he's noticed before you did. And thereafter you can never see that person without seeing those particular characteristics. Peter was very good at that. He did impressions of people that noboby else was doing – the chief one I remember was *Dick Barton* which we all took very seriously, and Peter was the first to catch on to the fact that it was impressionable.

Pat Dixon produced *Third Division* (1949) which Frank and I wrote and Peter was in it with all sorts of people, including Michael Bentine, Benny Hill (who was almost the straight man to Alfred Marks in those days), Patricia Hayes and Harry Secombe.

Pat Dixon was an extraordinary man. He had the American rebel flag on the wall of his office. Not only was he the first to stand behind the *Goon Show*, but he was also very instrumental in persuading the BBC to accept jazz programmes he'd put together. Of course, he and Spike and Peter shared a love for jazz.

When we came to do *Third Division* we used to write pastiche things for Peter, which is how 'Balham, Gateway to the South' came about. A few years ago, they wanted to start a Balham Carnival, rather like the Notting Hill Carnival, though it doesn't have the same ring. They asked Frank, who couldn't make it, and me to go along to the opening ceremony and so I went along not realizing how the piece had stuck somehow in the lining of people's minds. Beforehand they had put something in the *Evening Standard* about wanting to erect a statue to Peter for writing 'Balham' and putting it on the map, so we sent a letter which read:

'While we are all for putting up a statue to Peter Sellers, we may be able to save the good burghers of Balham a bit of money.

'It wasn't Sellers who dubbed the fair suburb, Gateway to the South. The sketch was one of several we wrote for him in *Third Division*, some of which he included in an album. However, this does not mean that Triangle Action Group must now involve itself in the expense of putting up *two* statues.

'For a trifling sum, we would be happy to go along to the new shopping centre and stand there personally.'

So our kinship with Balham continued for a long time.

Common Entrance and *So Little Time*, which Peter included on an LP, were also written for *Third Division*. We were on our mettle for that show because I can't tell you how grand the Third Programme was in those days, and being asked to write a comedy programme for it was like being asked to write an opera for Channel 5.

We also wrote something called *Finkel's Café,* which was a British version of a famous American Radio show. The premise was that people would go into a rather disreputable place in New York called Duffy's Tavern ('where the elite meet to eat'). We were asked to do an English version, and not only did it have good strong characters, but it offered great opportunities for star guests. Peter was Eddie, the manager of the café ('where the posh squash to nosh') who would always be very rude to the guests. Sidney James and Kenneth Connor were also in it. Peter decided that, as the American manager was very 'New Yoik', Eddie should be Irish. It was 1956, Pat Dixon produced again, and it ran for two series. It was funny because we would have these top-ranking guest stars then insult them.

When Peter became an actor he was still an impressionist. I remember him telling me once that for *There's A Girl in my Soup,* in which he played the part of a very fanciable toff, he was doing Patrick Lichfield. He was *being* Patrick Lichfield. Now, that may not have been 100 per cent impression, but the basis of it was, and then he plastered on various other characteristics demanded by the script. I've never seen him in anything since without trying to

Peter was usually happy to chat with the media – it was one of the trappings of fame

figure out who he was *being* and then adding on to it. Alec
Guinness was another protean actor, but he played a part by
becoming, say, an old woman, instead of becoming Irene Handl.
But both Frank and I felt that Peter was always a stunningly good
impressionist and that, with the possible exception of *Being There,*
you could do a bit of detective work to find out who he was doing.

Sometime in the sixties Peter came to me and said that he
wanted to do *Charley's Aunt* as a film. It was one of his
enthusiasms. He wanted it updated and he had Carlo Ponti
interested. I went over to where Peter was living in Italy. It was
while he was with Britt Ekland, and they were at the stage where
they were very good together. Which was nice. So I wrote a
treatment. He wanted it spiced up, so we decided that the Aunt
would still be from Brazil, 'Where the nuts come from', but she
would run a chain of brothels. He liked the idea of playing the
Aunt and the young man. I did a complete script and got very
involved with Carlo Ponti, and while we were arguing about it,
Carlo Ponti suddenly found out that he'd lost Peter from the
project, because another 'enthusiasm' had turned up.

That was Peter; it was wonderful while the stuff was all
floating in the air and was just an idea, but when it got down to the
nuts and bolts, he was off flying to some new castle in the air.
Similarly, long before that, we were going to do a radio series in
France with him. Pat Dixon went across and had a very pleasant
two weeks researching and eating and sampling the wine – but

when he got back, Peter was up, up and away again. He'd sort of apologize in an airy way. On the other hand I do recall that when I was doing a series called *Looks Familiar* he broke his arrangements in order to appear in it twice, which was good.

I recall he bought a car and he came round to show us. It was a Jeep looking thing. We asked him why he'd bought it and he said, 'It's got a spade on the front!' I asked him when he'd last used a spade, but that wasn't the point. After a couple of months he sold it. He lost money on every car he bought.

When I started on *It'll Be Alright on the Night* it was a touch and go venture because people didn't want to commit themselves to letting us show their out-takes in case it would make them look like lemons in the eyes of the public. I got hold of some out-takes of Peter's and I rang him up and asked if he'd got any objections and he said, 'No, no, fine.' Then, at the last minute, Blake Edwards announced he wasn't going to grant permission. So I rang Peter again and he said, 'Take no notice, just show them and I'll deal with Blake.' And he did. And once he had agreed to appearing we were then able to point out that Peter Sellers doesn't mind; and so we attracted some more actors in. The arrangement, incidentally, was that if the laughter was malicious we weren't going to transmit it. But it was affectionate laughter – the public found it endearing, and Peter really did have a giggle you couldn't resist; he just got you going – he was hopeless.

My perception of him as a man was that he was utterly

untrustworthy and entirely loveable: you couldn't put your money on him for anything. Then there was this sort of manic depressive thing which he shared with a lot of great comedians. This legend that comedians are sad men is not true, in my experience. Very often they are just solemn men; turgidly solemn. They take up on subjects earnestly. Peter had that, as well as a sudden manic mania. So that in the middle of it you'd hear the giggle and he'd be away with the fairies again! It's unforgivable if you haven't got any talent, but he had the talent to make it forgivable.

He was a good mate.

John P. Hamilton

John P. Hamilton worked on sound effects on the Goons.
He knew Peter for many years.

I first met Peter Sellers when I moved from Broadcasting House to Aeolian Hall in late 1949. Everyone met up sooner or later in the *gluepot* – otherwise the Grosvenor Arms – which was just around the corner from the Aeolian.

We first worked together on some of Dennis Main Wilson's Star Bill shows at the King's Theatre, Hammersmith, which was used as an Outside Broadcast venue. Peter and I had a number of things in common. We were both ex-RAF, both played drums and both mad about jazz. We therefore got on extremely well. We talked jazz a lot, swapped records occasionally and, in the days when he enjoyed fooling around with his cine camera, I helped him out with a few effects and things for the sound tracks.

After joining the team, my Sundays were fully occupied doing grams – sound effects and background noises – on the *Billy Cotton Band Show*, with early morning rehearsals and transmission at lunch-time, grabbing a quick bite and charging off to the Camden or Paris cinema, or wherever the Goons were being recorded, with cases full of bits and pieces from the Spot Effects store. After I defected from the Beeb in 1955 to become Head of Sound at Associated Rediffusion, we met up again on the *Fred* and *Son of Fred* shows (directed by Dick Lester). I did the sound balance, assisted by Sheila Blower and David Law, and we had a marvellous time on that very hilarious series. The Reg Owen group who provided the music had some of the best British jazz musicians including the great Phil Seamen on drums.

A tenuous connection I have with Peter makes me particularly proud. In one of the *Fred* sketches, Peter did his Richard the Third bit. 'Now is the Winter of our discontent ...' etc. He finished it with one of his great ad libs in that series which went: 'And can I do all this, and still not get a *Worker's Playtime?*' It was funny in the context of the age when a lot of people still remembered the wartime radio shows of which *Worker's Playtime* was one. For the part, the make-up department had acquired the actual wig that Laurence Olivier had worn in the movie of Richard III. About a year later, I played the King in an in-house pantomime of the Sleeping Beauty, and wore the self-same wig. I have a video of that show, and when I look at it think, 'Cor! Look at me in that wig. Olivier, Sellers and me.' What an honour.

In 1959 I became a Producer/Director at A-R, and Peter's and my paths didn't cross again until 1968, when I was about to move to LWT, after A-R lost its franchise. I had a call from Peter Eton (freelance producer at the time) who told me he had done a deal with the new Thames TV to shoot a visual version of a *Goon Show* for transmission in the first week of the new company's weekday slots. He asked me if I'd like to relive my past and do the spot effects for the show. I got the necessary go-ahead, and so, one Sunday in June, we all met up again in Studio One at Teddington and got down to rehearsing with Joe McGrath, who was directing.

The set-up is captured in a publicity photograph taken by the staff photographer at Thames, and used as the front cover – some years later – by EMI, when they released the LP, *The Very Best of the Goons – Vol 1.* The show we recorded is not part of that LP. It was one that I had worked on for the radio series and that Spike had re-written for this TV version. *Tales of Men's Shirts* was essentially the same as the original, and we all had a hilarious day with everbody on good form. It was helped along by the fact that Peter brought a couple of cases of fine wines with him, which we hid behind the central flat seen in that cover picture, and which took a bashing through the day and right up to recording time.

When my wife, Daphne Shadwell, arrived for the show, she knew I'd been drinking and spent the evening wondering if I would get everything right! All was well. And the audience was excellent, loving every minute. The show was recorded on video for Thames's use, and on film for Peter Eton Productions to have a marketable copy for world-wide sales. Without getting too technical, that system – known as Gemini – was unique at that time, and a copy of the show was ordered, some years later, by the then IBA to go into their archives.

My last meeting with Peter was in the early Seventies, when we met, by chance, in Marylebone High Street, right outside Henekeys hostelry. It was a Monday morning, and I was on my way to the bank, and Peter was on his way to see his agent. On the corner of the street opposite the pub, a shop was being rebuilt, surrounded with scaffolding and a number of workmen. As we stopped to chat one of the workmen spotted Peter and started bellowing in goon-like voices to the street below. The others joined in and, I have to say, their impressions were not bad at all. Peter couldn't resist the challenge and started back at them. This bellowed battle of words went on for some minutes, much to the amusement of passers-by, and people in the pub who came out to see what was going on. In the end, and with me in hysterics, we both went into the pub and upstairs to the winebar. We had a half-bottle of champagne, some sane chat and parted company.

An odd tailpiece to this happened just a few weeks ago (I'm

writing this in November '99), when Daphne and I popped into a small Italian restaurant in Dorset Street, just off Baker Street. It was quite late, and as we walked to our table, a soft Scottish voice called over: 'Hey! Good God, I havenae seen you two in years! Remember me? I'm Charles. I used to run the wine bar at Henekeys.'

And so it was; and he recalled the incident in all its details – twenty-five or so years later.

But mine, and others' memories of Peter Sellers will last much, much longer than that.

Kenneth Branagh

The actor, Kenneth Branagh, recalls an early memory of Peter.

I was mesmerized at watching Peter Sellers as Olivier as Richard III, on what I think was a Sunday night variety programme in my youth. He shared with Olivier the uncommon gift of being funny and sexy at one and the same time.

He is partly to blame for my Shakespearean career!

Sir Peter Hall

Sir Peter Hall directed Peter Sellers in the stage play *Brouhaha* in 1958. The following contribution comes from an *Arena* documentary in the life of Peter Sellers – called *The Peter Sellers Story* – first transmitted in 1995 on BBC2.

Peter, in some respects, was as good an actor as Alec Guinness, or as good an actor as Laurence Olivier. He had the ability to identify completely with another person and think his way physically and mentally and emotionally into their skin. Where does that come from? I have no idea. Is it a curse? Often. I don't think there is a correlation which is direct, though. I think it's not enough to have talent – you have to have another talent to handle that talent and that, I think, Peter did not have. I think he was a genius, and I think his perfectionism made him extremely neurotic, extremely selfish. I'm sure the play or the film was only about *him* in *his* view. It is no good arguing with that; that's the nature of that kind of psyche.

Michael Sellers

Composer Henry Mancini liked a puff on the weed, and usually had a smoke with him at all times. My father said to him, 'But what about Customs when you're travelling?' With a shrug he replied, 'Who's going to bust the man who wrote *Moon River*!'

Nicholas Parsons

The actor/straight man/presenter, Nicholas Parsons, appeared with Peter in *Carlton-Browne of the FO* (1958).

My impression of Peter was of a shy man who handled it by being extrovert in front of an audience. I saw him, at the Palladium doing impersonations. At the time, I thought his acting was OTT and eccentric. However, during the course of the Goons Peter's acting became more subtle. Some aspects of the Goons were subtle and it gave Peter a chance to refine his acting.

I worked on *Carlton-Browne of the FO* with the Boulting Brothers, and Peter was in it. The Boultings were patient perfectionists and brought out some good performances from Peter. I recall learning that Roy Boulting persuaded Peter to do him and his brother a favour by doing a dummy run as Fred Kite in *I'm All Right, Jack* and when Peter saw it he agreed to do the part.

He certainly was an inspirational performer and it seems to me that he was in touch with the child within himself, which people involved in comedy need to be. Now, this may have caused problems with his family and friends, but it made him great.

In my opinion, Peter was a comic genius and that lay in his ability to underplay. Although comedy needs broad strokes his subtlety was his genius.

Peter in Carlton-Browne of the F.O.

Ian Carmichael

The actor Ian Carmichael worked with Peter in
I'm All Right, Jack (1959).

I remember Peter as an instantaneous person. He did his best work
on take one – whereas most actors need more. Terry Thomas was
bad on his lines and couldn't remember them. His scenes,
including those with Peter, ran into many takes, but Peter, then,
was disciplined and never lost his temper that I saw. And he and
Terry Thomas were friends.

I never found Peter difficult during *I'm All Right, Jack.* He
was very fond of Irene Handl, who played his wife, and enjoyed
her company. I think the fact that she worked on some of his LPs
shows his respect for her.

Peter also respected the Boulting Brothers. The shooting
schedule was ten weeks and I don't recall any giggling. I think
that's because it was comedy and not farce, and Peter's Goon
humour was not moulded into it. It was very different from the
comedy he had been doing.

At weekends, Peter would call me up and ask me over to see a
movie. I lived quite near him and Anne at the time. He had built
himself an attic cinema, and he would ask me which film I wanted
to see, and I would say *Funny Face* or *The Glenn Miller Story,* and
that's what we would watch. It was very pleasant.

He had this tape recorder, which was the latest technology,

and he would record his voice: sometimes he would sing and play his ukelele, then he would play it back at the wrong speed, like Jimmy Young used to do with 'What's the recipe today, Jim?' That made Peter laugh – and so did Spike Milligan and the Goons.

Bryan Forbes

The following piece on Peter Sellers first appeared in *A Divided Life* (Heinemann, 1992), the autobiography of the writer/director/actor Bryan Forbes.

Once Peter Sellers latched on to a comic idea, he loved nothing more than to carry it to extremes. There was an occasion when he, Nannette (Nanette Newman, actress, and Mrs Bryan Forbes) and I decided to go to Paris for a long weekend. We were spotted at London airport by a young and naïve reporter from the then *Daily Sketch*. What was the purpose of our trip? Peter immediately began to invent. 'Mr Forbes and I are going to Paris to sign up a new pop star we've discovered.'

The reporter grabbed his notebook. 'Is this exclusive?'

'Absolutely. You're the first person we've told.'

'Can I have his name?'

Peter was inspired. 'Turk Thrust,' he said.

'Turk Thrust?' The stub of the pencil scribbled furiously. 'Is that his real name?'

'It is now. He had it changed by Deed Poll.'

'And are you going to manage him?'

'We hope to. He's going to be big, really big. Bigger than Freda Clench.'

I felt Peter had now gone too far, but the reporter swallowed it whole.

'I can't tell you how grateful I am, Mr Sellers, Mr Forbes. This is a big break for me. Don't give it to anybody else, will you?'

'It's all yours.'

We flew off well pleased with ourselves, had a hilarious weekend and returned home to find that the *Sketch* had given the story a lot of space.

'We must keep Turk Thrust alive,' Peter said. 'He's too good to kill off quickly.'

We organized a fake LP complete with lurid sleeve cover and titled TURK THRUST'S GREATEST HITS. Much to our amazement nobody saw through the deception. We continued to build on the legend. I made an appearance in Peter's *A Shot in the Dark* as a nude guitarist suitably disguised with a beard and billed on the screen as Turk. Nanette appeared on television's *Juke-Box Jury* and when asked for her opinion of a new single said, 'I like it but I think I prefer the Turk Thrust version.' The presenter nodded in agreement. 'Yes,' he said, 'a lot of other people have said that.'

At one time we considered finding an unknown singer and

grooming him for the role. Given the name, and the idiocy of much of the pop scene, he might have actually made a career.

I felt the loss of Peter as keenly as anybody and scarcely a week goes by without some fond memory of him surfacing. He was an emotional, perennial nomad, both on and off screen, often, I thought, consumed with doubts about his ability to sustain success, either soaring high on the peaks or else plunged in the valleys;

Peter receives ideas from Blake Edwards while Elke Sommer looks on.
A Shot in the Dark, *1964*

there was no in between. A confirmed hopeless romantic, he could never resist falling in love and would immediately shower the object of his affections with the most lavish gifts. Such interludes often took bizarre turns as Nanette and I once experienced. Nanette was his leading lady in a comedy called *The Wrong Arm of the Law* and half-way through the shooting Peter said he needed to talk to me on a highly personal matter. He came to the house and took up a pose in front of our sitting room fireplace.

'You know you're one of my oldest and closest friends, don't you?' he began.

'Of course, Pete.'

'And you know I'd never go behind your back or willingly do anything to hurt you?'

'Of course.'

Having established that, he went straight to the heart of the matter. 'I want to marry Nanette.'

It was a difficult bombshell to duck, but once I had recovered from the shock I tried to reply with the gravity the situation demanded.

'Well, obviously I can't fault your taste, Pete,' I said. 'How does Nanette feel about it?'

'I haven't told her yet. I thought it right to tell you first.'

'I appreciate that.'

The scene had taken on the characteristics of a Pinter play but I knew it would be a mistake to appear outraged or to mock him: that was not the way to handle Peter. The situation called for delicacy.

'I know it comes as a great surprise to you, but I've fallen in love and I have to be honest about it.'

'Well, I understand,' I said. 'I happen to love her myself. What d'you think we should do about it?'

'We'll still remain friends, nothing will change that.' It dawned on me that Peter was not entertaining failure. He had convinced himself that once he had made the confession to me and I had accepted the inevitable all would revert to the status quo. To him it was a new role to play, a new mask to wear, and he saw nothing odd in it.

'I think it'd be best if I told Nanette, don't you?' I said, hoping that Nanette would not come into the room at that moment.

'Yes, I think that's probably a good idea. Break it to her gently. How d'you think she'll take it?'

'She'll obviously be flattered, and I know she's very fond of you.' I managed to keep mounting hysteria out of my voice. To have laughed at Peter at that point would have invited disaster. He was so patently sincere and desperate to do the right thing according to his unique code of ethics. 'I guess we'll just have to wait and see. Of course, there's the children to take into account.'

'You'd always be able to see them,' Peter said, relaxed and reasonable now, as though the conversation we were having was everyday stuff. 'Will you stay on here?'

'Difficult to say. I love it here, so does Nanette,' I ended lamely, by now infected with his madness and at a loss to make any further sense of the comedy we were embarked upon.

'You're not angry, are you?'

'Angry? No, I appreciate you being so open about it.'

Nanette joined us at that point and for the rest of the evening the subject was never mentioned. We all had a perfectly normal evening together with Peter on top form.

Thus began two very strange years. I doubt if they come any stranger.

Peter had made up his mind that his destiny lay with Nanette and the role he had selected had to be played out with a straight face.

When we were alone later that same evening I told Nanette Peter's confession and intentions. We both agreed that we had to tread very carefully if an old friendship we both valued was not to go up in flames. One could not mock Peter, that would have been too cruel, for despite his fame he was always vulnerable to criticism. At that point we both felt it was just another of his infatuations which would die a natural death. We had lived through his first divorce, brought about by his conviction that he was in love with Sophia Loren, and we had held his hand while he suffered numerous other emotional setbacks. I had been honest when I said I wasn't angry with him. He was what he was, often confused, given to wild enthusiasms that usually disappeared overnight.

Opposite:

Peter in The Wrong Arm of the Law, *1963, during which he fell in love with Nanette Newman*

But we were both wrong on this occasion. His obsession with Nanette did not follow the familiar pattern. He was deadly serious and my first reaction to his bombshell had been a mistake. It fell to Nanette to handle the situation alone as best she could and she handled it brilliantly, never hurting his feelings, but gently pointing out the impossibility of the situation. Peter was nothing if not persistent and could not admit defeat, but there were moments when he was forced to see the farcical side of it all. Even at this far remove, I am conscious that as I set down the sequence of events the entire episode must appear unbelievable to outsiders. Yet we remained the best of friends, for Nanette adored Peter as a companion and throughout all the twists and turns of this innocent *ménage à trois* she handled his many ploys with gentle tact that sprang from a real affection for him and an understanding of his troubled, mercurial nature. How she did it and remained sane was quite remarkable for Peter's moods could veer this way and that at a moment's notice. On two occasions he brought a gun and threatened suicide and both times Nanette somehow calmed him and talked him out of it. Then there would be periods when Peter was rational and would acknowledge the hopelessness of the situation, followed by periods when he would use every artifice in his considerable repertoire to gain his ends.

We lived through seasons of unreality never quite knowing which ploy Peter would try next. One day he would attempt to buy Nanette the most expensive gifts, furs and jewellery, but always tell me beforehand and ask if I objected. When Nanette refused them, he could not understand her refusal. He pleaded to accompany us on holidays, and more than once I felt we were players in a triangle written by Coward. For two whole years we were held captive by his relentless obsession.

I have no reason to suppose that his affection for Nanette was anything other than genuine and, although the situation often became nightmarish, I could never take lasting offence because he was so open about his intentions. Nothing Peter ever did was conventional. To be his friend, one had to accept that life would be full of surprises; some good, some difficult to take, but always possible to forgive. His emotions were always on the surface, nothing was ever hidden. Eventually, of course, his ardour, denied consummation, gradually lost potency like wine diluted with water. He went on to remarry three more times, seeking the perfect bluebird of happiness that sadly always eluded him.

Whatever his marital and emotional failures, Peter's artistry, so closely encircled within his volatile temperament, went far beyond some ill-founded criticism of his worth as an actor. Because his rise to world fame started with the *Goon Show* he was often written off as a gifted mimic. I totally disagree. He was a great film artist, and the characters he invented seemed to rise effortlessly from a deep well of invention. But the effort, in fact, was enormous, the artistry concealed the struggle he always underwent before starting a new role. But once the character was firmly in his grasp (as with his immortal Clouseau) he became possessed, delighted with the discovery in the way small boys are delighted when they find out how a toy works. He was at his best when he could efface his own personality beneath a disguise; on such occasions he was without equal. He made mistakes, he made bad films, and he was not always the best judge of material. But he gave to the screen a gallery of original portraits – the shop steward in *I'm All Right, Jack*, all his roles in *Dr Strangelove,* the old general in *The Waltz of the Toreadors,* the gardener in *Being There* and a superb vignette for me as the venal Doctor Pratt overwhelmed by cats and death certificates in *The Wrong Box*: in only two short scenes he served up the quintessence of what made him a unique performer.

There was a fat man always struggling to get out of Peter and his constant longing to be a romantic leading man contributed, in my opinion, to the sadness behind the clown's mask he presented to the world at large, and hastened his death.

Now, when the memories of those years of madness have faded, we constantly remember the hilarious escapades we shared for when the good times rolled there was no more generous or enchanting companion.

Herbert Lom

The actor, Herbert Lom, knew and worked with Peter for many years. It is for his role as Clouseau's boss in the Pink Panther movies that he is most fondly remembered throughout the world.

When we were making *The Ladykillers* Peter was driving a brand new red Bentley Continental, and we painted a fake scratch the whole length of it. It looked like it had been hit by a lorry! When Peter saw it he was horrified and covered his face with his hands; but as he approached, he realized what it was and that it would wash off, and we confessed.

A couple of days later, I started my own Bentley and drove home from Ealing to London. I noticed a smell of kippers. I couldn't understand where it was coming from, and eventually I

Herbert Lom as Dreyfuss, undergoing counselling to help cope with Clouseau

Charles Haslett as Inspector Clouseau. He earns his living as a look-alike. Interest in Clouseau today is as strong as ever and he has to learn the films by heart to keep up with the public

took it into a garage to be examined. The man looked under the engine and found that there, pinned expertly with wire, were kippers. Every time I'd started that engine the kippers had been grilling. Peter's revenge!

I remember I had nut cutlets with Peter in Hollywood, then I met him in London and he ordered steak. I asked him, 'What happened to being a vegetarian?' He replied, 'I went off it!'

One day he came round to my house and he was very

depressed. Eventually, I found out the reason why. He had been offered a serious Shakespearean play at Stratford and he was confused by the offer. He didn't know who he was and it depressed him: he was unsure as to whether he should or should not accept the role. When he told me I took five seconds and told him to throw it away; he was a great comedy actor and shouldn't consider doing Shakespeare. It was as if a weight lifted off his shoulders. He was suddenly in a good mood and drank some wine. He turned down the offer.

He had a house built in the western part of the South of France, and while waiting for it to be completed he took a villa to supervise the decoration etc. I rang him the day he moved in to wish him good luck, and he said, 'We're moving out.' He went on, 'We don't like it and we don't like the French.' I asked him why not. He replied, 'They can't speak English.' A week later the house was on the market.

Peter could be a funny man as well as funny on the screen. I remember in Paris (we must have been staying there filming something) in an hotel, he had us all laughing by impersonating the Americans and getting the French pronunciation all wrong.

My twitch in the Pink Panthers started because Peter ad-libbed a wink at me. My character was miserable and he winked to cheer me up. I winked back but as my nerves were stronger than I was I went on winking for about thirty seconds! The director (Blake Edwards) said, 'Keep that in.'

Roy Hudd

Comedy actor and familiar voice on the radio, Roy Hudd
makes the following observations.

I think what made Peter Sellers special was his transition from variety
turn to voices man on the radio to superb comedy actor. This
doesn't happen very often as the powers that be do tend to pigeon-
hole performers. Peter never allowed this to happen but seemed to
me, as an observer, to always be stretching himself – for ever
searching for the next character. He did become the characters he
created; his creations were never just cartoons, they were real people.

My favourite film was *I'm All Right, Jack* and I think his performance
in that was my favourite, too. I know people who are like that.

He was the master with the Goons. Spike was the inspiration.
Harry played the Kenneth Horne, Roy Hudd part (himself), but
Peter created the wonderful characters that are so remembered. He
somehow made the lunatic words he had to say sound logical.

It is impossible to explain his mastery. Perhaps it had something
to do with his show business background. Certainly he was a
wonderful sponge. All sorts of idiosyncrasies of speech, movement
and appearance were stored away in his memory to be brought out
when he had to create a character.

His brilliant work has only made me try even harder to follow in
his footsteps. I try with only a tiny percentage of his observation, wit
and creativity.

David Jacobs

Radio and TV presenter, David Jacobs, recalls Peter's
train-set fixation.

Peter was a compulsive shopper and bought the whole catalogue
of Hornby Double O train sets. Later, he told me he had made
a mistake and he offered me the sets, in their boxes, for £150,
when they were worth over £1,000. I said no to him as, at the time,
my son and I were collecting and buying them one a week and it
would have spoiled that. So Peter sold them to Graham Stark.

Michael Sellers

Everyone must remember *The Muppet Show*. My father had
been asked to appear in the show, but had declined as he
didn't have a clue what they were all about. I was at his flat one
evening and mentioned that it was time for the Muppets on TV. It
was then he told me he'd been asked to appear on the show. I
convinced him to sit down and watch it and he did and loved it –
particularly Fozzy Bear. The next day, he booked himself on the
show. I had to go along to see him record, of course – just to see
my favourite: Animal.

Burt Kwouk

Actor Burt Kwouk appeared in all but the first Panther film. He also appeared in two James Bond films and now works with Harry Hill.

I learned a lot from Peter, particularly how to be 'second banana' – by which I mean like a straight man to him. Over a period of time you learn how to work with someone and out of that came: 'Peter top banana, Burt second banana'. I used to absorb things by watching and working with Peter, it was like osmosis. For example, I kept still while he was acting, it became automatic and after a while I didn't even realize I was doing it

On our first Clouseau film together, *A Shot in the Dark* (1964), I couldn't get something right, I forget what now, but I became very despondent and went and sat in a corner. I was quiet there when I felt a hand on my shoulder and there was Clouseau's face looking down into mine. 'That's all right, Burt,' he said 'none of us can do it.' Actually that was very unlike Peter because he wasn't the most aware person in the world! Often he wouldn't have noticed but he did on this occasion.

Sometimes Peter would say, 'That's not very funny' to me but he wouldn't tell me how to do it. I had to work it out for myself and it was much better for me to discover it that way, much more effective. He didn't impose his ideas on me of how to make something funny, it probably wouldn't have worked if another person had done it. In fact, Peter never imposed himself as a star.

As the Pink Panther pictures became bigger so his performance became broader, the Clouseau accent became more outrageous and so did the disguises.

The relationship between Blake and Peter could be pretty fiery; each wanted to be king. The Pink Panther had been Blake's creation but Clouseau was Peter's creation (after the part had been intended for Peter Ustinov) and both had a different vision of how their creation fitted in. But conflict is useful; it sparks off some good stuff.

There were good times and bad times on the films but I thoroughly enjoyed working on them. I remember once Peter and Blake were arguing about make-up and the colour of Peter's skin. Blake asked me, 'What colour are you wearing?' I answered, 'Yellow!' They both laughed and the situation was relieved. No, I didn't invent being his 'little yellow friend' – that was already in the script.

There was quite a bit of ad-libbing in the films, particularly the physical bits which are so difficult to script. In *The Return of the Pink Panther* (1975) the scenes with the hoover, the parrot and the light bulb were largely spur of the moment. There was a lot of debate before shooting the physical humour about what could come next and whether we had done it before.

I recall that when we returned from shooting in Hong Kong

for the last Pink Panther Peter made, *The Revenge of the Pink Panther* (1978), it was so cold when we stepped of the plane in Britain that Blake and Peter decided to shoot in the South of France instead.

He was a friend but after he went abroad to live because of the tax situation we saw less of each other, although we always stayed friends. He certainly didn't like living away from England, he hated being away from his cronies, people like Spike Milligan.

After Peter had his heart attacks in 1964, we were all aware of his health condition. He didn't make an issue of it, although he did

Peter's second role in his final film – Nayland Smith in The Fiendish Plot of Dr Fu Manchu

become volatile which may have had something to do with it. However, I never noticed any problems, neither did I notice a deterioration in him. We always had doubles around to perform the tricky stuff, so if Peter couldn't do it it didn't show anyway. However, I did always have his health at the back of my mind somehow. I was only three years younger than him. It is difficult now not to look back with hindsight but at the time I really didn't think he looked unhealthy. Even on *The Fiendish Plot of Dr Fu Manchu* (1980) which turned out to be his last film. You see, he was always changing his appearance for a film, putting on weight, losing it and so on; he was a chameleon. Therefore, when I saw him for that last film I thought he was looking that way in order to play the characters in it. The film did get out of control and Peter became the governor on it.

It was a great shock to me when he died because he didn't seem unhealthy. However, heart attacks can hit without someone being unhealthy. I had no idea whether he was on medication or not and he didn't seem to let it affect his life, as far as I could see. Blake, who used to smoke heavily, became terribly anti-smoking and it wasn't allowed anywhere on the stage. Having said that, I can't say I was surprised when Peter died because for years his heart problems had been in the background and he had told me, 'I'm living on borrowed time.'

I was very fond of him and I missed him after he died – I still do miss him. After all, it was a large chunk of my life.

Françoise Pascal

The actress, Françoise Pascal, worked with Peter Sellers and Goldie Hawn in the 1971 film *There's a Girl in my Soup*.

Opposite:

Peter as a

Japanese officer in

Soft Beds, Hard

Battles, *1974. He*

had a life-size

stand-up photo of

his character put

in Burt Kwouk's

dressing-room as

a joke

I was living with my then boyfriend of three years (Richard Johnson) and, in February 1970, I had discovered that I was pregnant. I was only twenty years old and I was very excited about it.

On 21 February 1970, we had lunch at the Dell 'Arcthusa on the King's Road with Warren Beatty, Roman Polanski, Vivianne Ventura, Victor Lowndes and others. After lunch I went to Vivianne's house to learn how to knit for the new baby, and whilst I was there a fire broke out from an electrical fault in the basement of her house, and I found myself engulfed with black smoke. I became increasingly conscious that I could not get out after Vivianne had told me to follow her. I could not breathe and decided to open the window – a fatal mistake! I stood on the window ledge of the third floor of her house and saw many people on the street, including Roman Polanski and Gene Gutowsky (film producer) who held a sheet for me to jump on. I jumped, missed the sheet, and ended up on some iron railings, with my neck between two of the railings and my left arm impaled on another.

I was taken, unconscious, to St George's Hospital in Belgravia which I lived behind with Richard in Grosvenor Crescent Mews. I was put in a ward and, being under morphine, had no idea who came and who went.

On my second day in hospital, I vaguely remembered this Indian doctor coming to see me (I was drugged to the eyeballs!), sitting by my bed and talking to me. When I eventually woke up (my fourth day in hospital) I saw one rose and a card. They were from Peter, who had apparently spent a whole afternoon at my side telling jokes, and dressed as an Indian doctor so as not to be recognized by the press.

On the card were written these lovely words: Get well soon, as I wish to say to you again, MY GOD BUT YOU'RE LOVELY.

Those words were from the film *There's a Girl in my Soup.*

The thoughtfulness of this man was tremendous, and he gave me a will to get up and get better. Three days later I was out of hospital with a broken arm and a dislocated left shoulder. Peter telephoned several times to enquire about my health. I will never forget his kindness towards me in those hard times. Needless to say, I had lost the baby and he was very sympathetic.

I co-starred in his next film, *Soft Beds, Hard Battles*, on his request.

I was mortified when he died as I was on stage in Edinburgh doing *Happy Birthday*, and could not get back to London. I sent Lynne Frederick flowers and my condolences but she never replied.

Peter was a marvellous man. I sat many evenings with him in his flat in Belgravia, listening to his Indian music and listening to him talking in an Indian voice, and generally having a good laugh.

I used to see him very relaxed, and he was great to be with. I loved him to bits as a friend and miss his sense of humour and his kindness.

Another of Peter's roles – Hitler in Soft beds, Hard Battles

In costume for The Magician of Lublin, *which Peter never actually made*

Fiona Fullerton

Actress, Fiona Fullerton, played Alice to Peter Sellers' March Hare in *Alice In Wonderland*, 1972.

Peter and Dudley Moore seemed to hit it off straight away. Perhaps this was because they were both playing furry animals with big teeth! Robert Helpmann, who played the Mad Hatter, was rather left out as Peter (as the March Hare) and Dudley (the Dormouse) leapt around the set twirling their long tails and pulling funny faces. The teeth caused much hilarity as they kept falling out, and Peter insisted on eating his lunch with them in! The two were so funny together, that I just remember laughing and laughing for the whole four days it took to shoot the tea-party scene.

If you look at the song, I am laughing spontaneously as Peter does something crazy on the table. He hated rehearsing the dance, which irritated Bobby Helpmann, so we kept re-shooting the number over and over.

Peter and Dudley loved their costumes and behaved like naughty schoolboys in them. They even went to the local pub near Shepperton Studios wearing them. The idea of strolling down the street dressed as a hare appealed greatly to Peter.

Goldie Hawn was on the set a lot with Peter, so she could have been his girlfriend at the time. I remember talking to her about being ballet dancers – which we both were.

I adored Peter and thought him very funny, and when he

Michael Sellers

I recall very clearly the time I visited my father on the set of Alice in Wonderland – with a very young Fiona Fullerton as Alice. My father was playing the March Hare. (See photo.) The costume had a string to lower the ears. At lunch we decided to go to a local pub, so off we went, with him driving the Mercedes. The looks we got when people saw the March Hare driving around the countryside in a Mercedes was hilarious. The drinks and the meal which followed make me laugh even now. And this was one occasion when he definitely didn't get recognized!

Spike was playing the Griffin. He didn't come with us to lunch, because the costume he was wearing was so extreme he could hardly walk and was only able to drink through a straw.

turned up at the Royal Premiere for *Alice* in London – we were all presented to HM the Queen – he had his hand bandaged up. I asked him, 'What have you done to it?'

'Oh, nothing,' he replied. 'It's just to avoid clapping!'

Kenneth Griffith

The renowned actor Kenneth Griffith was a close friend of Peter. The following observations are taken from his autobiography *The Fool's Pardon* (Little, Brown,1994).

The creative or character actor actually has the ability to move his own established personality to become – to change into – whatever the author or, indeed, history has engraved. Few players have achieved stardom through doing it – in America before the war, Paul Muni; and in Britain Alec Guinness and Peter Sellers.

Amongst the catalogue of routine jobs that paved my path at that time was a film called *The Naked Truth* (1958). Also in it, playing the lead role, was a chap named Peter Sellers. I had met him once before while walking up Shaftesbury Avenue, and David Jacobs introduced us. At that time, Peter was becoming well known through his radio work. I remember that he was warm towards me. It was the beginning of a friendship which only wavered once, and briefly, to the end of his days.

If you were acceptable in Peter's mind, you entered a world of profit and delight, occasionally punctuated by an opportunity to share his despair. I suppose he could have been called a manic-depressive, but for me, most of the time, it was vivid fun and more laughs than I have been given anywhere else. But there was much more to Peter Sellers than humour. One day, after lunch, I joined the key members of the film unit at the daily 'rushes' – the viewing of the previous day's work. Of course, on those professional occasions, everyone stares critically at his or her own contribution. I cannot recall what exactly distressed me about my own performance, but as soon as I could escape from that little viewing theatre, I hastened to the deserted sound-stage (where we filmed) in a state of shock and muttering to myself, 'Never do *THAT* again!' But the sound-stage was not empty. Peter Sellers was already there, prowling, with a terrible scowl on his face. Full of shame, I edged towards him and muttered contritely, 'What did you think of the rushes?'

He snarled an angry, 'What do you think I bloody well thought? Dreadful!'

I felt I deserved this extreme flagellation, but was taken aback at the merciless degree of his vehemence.

'Well,' I mumbled, 'I'll never do *THAT* again.'

'What?' he said, confused.

'Well, at least I saw what I did and I've learnt a hard lesson.'

'What?' repeated Sellers.

'Well, I *KNOW* I was dreadful in that dressing-room scene.'

'Dreadful?' he roared. 'You were bloody marvellous! *I* was dreadful! And you being so marvellous made it worse, Kenny.'

Whoever was right or wrong, it was clear that we both cared passionately.

Soon after, the Boulting Brothers made their monumentally prophetic and hilarious film *I'm All Right, Jack.* The highlight of my own experience on the film was in a scene where my mentally backward character (we were the same people we had been in *Private's Progress,* but now in civvy street) goes up to Mr Kite's (PS's) office to report the frightening fact that Stanley Windrush (Ian Carmichael) was happily putting in an honest day's work. Fred Kite hears this appalling story, which cuts across everything that the British Trade Union Movement stood for, and nodding approval to his cronies – which included the actor Cardew Robinson – says of my character: 'A promising lad, this!'

And when I had performed my short sycophantic piece, Peter Sellers clapped his hands in applause. I mention this memory because of *HIS* opinion in front of the team. What an accolade! Peter Sellers always treated me as a peer and, for me, his opinion was one of the few that truly counted.

Peter Sellers on *Desert Island Discs*

Broadcast 4/2/57

I Want A Big Butter and Egg Man – Bobby Hackett and his Jazz
    Band

I Have Dreamed – Rita Moreno/Carlos Rivas

On Hearing the First Cuckoo in Spring – Delius – LSO conducted
    by Collins

Cheek to Cheek – Ella Fitzgerald/Louis Armstrong

La Fille aux Cheveux de Lin – Debussy – Hans Henkemans, piano

White – Young – from *Tone Poems of Colour*, conducted by Frank
    Sinatra

Laura (from the film) – Erroll Garner, piano

I Like to Recognize the Tune – Mel Torme

Luxury Item – A snorkel outfit

Book – *The Pickwick Papers*, Charles Dickens

'Style' List 1967

Peter was asked, for a fee, to 'say what you believe has that indefinable something called style.' He agreed because he liked the idea – and he did it for nothing.

PETER'S LIST

My wife
A red Lamborghini Miura
El Cordobes
Private Eye magazine
Habit Rouge de Guerlain
Leicaflex and Summicron – Rf/2 50mm
Elmarit – Rf/2.8 35mm Elmarit – R2.8 90mm
The music of Antonio Carlos Jobim
A Baglietto 18m motor-yacht
The *Daily Mirror*
Hi-fi
Vodka
Shakespeare
Sid Perelman
Roast beef and Yorkshire pudding
Italian shoes
Some Chinese food
Fred

A final word by Spike Milligan

Taken from the 1969 BBC programme, *Will the Real Peter Sellers…'*, quoted by permission of Spike Milligan. These words, spoken by one of his closest friends, come as close as anything to explaining the contradictions at the heart of Peter's character.

Will the real Peter Sellers stand up? Not until he's dead. Peter frequently stretches out his hand to try and help someone. The trouble is that he knows that every living thing will eventually drag him down. He sees himself as a clean person in a colony of lepers and he can't afford to mix with them too much if he's to come out clean again. He knows that within him is such a large area of unexplored emotionalism that he can't afford to take any risks if he is to survive. If he did, he'd spill out all his emotions to such an extent that he'd drown himself.

Peter's biggest rage is that he can't be violent. But don't

mistake it – he's FULL of rage! The rage of a murderer and yet he's too kind and too good to actually knife anybody. But just suppose he did . . . he'd be free now.

He cries for yesterday and this has made him very lonely. This constant journeying is at the essence of it, like a panther in a cage, pacing backwards and forwards, for eternity. Peter's isolated. He's that lonely now. For Peter, life is just a terrible journey. He daren't stand still because he'd sink into the mire of his past, he'd drown himself in his own tears, so he has to keep going although he knows he's got nowhere to go BUT he's making the journey with all guns going and all flags flying. If there'd been a luggage compartment on Apollo 11 to the moon, Sellers would have been in it.

Wherever he is he thinks, 'It's boring'. Isn't that a terrible crucifix he has to bear? Can you imagine the agony of it if he hadn't made it financially? I think he'd have killed himself.

We had to create the *Goon Show*. In a fantasy world you always win because you are writing the script. You can't get arrested in a fantasy unless you want it. So for anyone who found reality a bug, like Peter did, the *Goon Show* was sheer therapy. Neddie Seagoon was all the idiots Peter hated. He could be struck, clubbed, burned, drowned, boiled and nailed to a cross and Peter would love it! For him the characters were real and they came alive. For years he has stuck idiots: idiot producers who have ruined wonderful material, idiot managers who told him he

couldn't act, idiot BBC officials who treated him like a naughty boy. And he won't take it any more. So the *Goon Show* liberated us all.

Peter's tragedy was that he was a singular talent who became caught up in a collective art. He realized that he had to go into films (even if the film world did contain more idiots than anywhere else) in order to get enough money to make his *Goon Show* revenge actually happen. If we'd have been an organization we'd have been raided in the night, knock on the door, next day prison.

*'Wait till you see the full effect in the hurmp!'.
Clouseau's hunchback disguise in* The Pink Panther Strikes Again, *1976*

But you can't arrest an attitude of mind and Peter IS that attitude of mind. In getting to that position, however, he suffered terribly.

The only thing that doesn't get him down are his gadgets, like his cameras. Strange that he should have chosen photography – the art of loneliness in pursuit of the lonely.

He's probably one of the greatest living actors if only someone would let him act and stop expecting him to do the funnies all the time.

Being with his children are the least unhappy moments in his life and so he classifies them as happiness.

The pity of it all.

Peter's nightmares are our nightmares too. His ghosts, our ghosts. He's Mr I Don't Know of the Twentieth Century. He IS Mr Twentieth Century.

Good night, sweet prince, may angels watch over you.

Opposite: Peter with his daughter, Sarah

Peter with his camera, in Paris in 1980

INDEX OF CONTRIBUTORS

The publisher would like to thank Bryan Forbes and Heinemann for the use of his piece, Kenneth Griffith and Little, Brown for the use of his contribution and Spike Milligan and the BBC for the use of 'A Final Word from Spike Milligan'.

PICTURE LIST

©BBC: 8, 114-15
©Howard L. Bingham: 4, 106
©Theo Cowan Ltd: 5, 10, 57, 122, 155, 176
©Charles Haslett: 164
©London Features: 190-1
©Photonews Ltd: 18-19
©Rex Features: 27, 32, 75, 85, 188
©Tazio Secchiaroli: 88
©David Sim: 6
©Solo: 57, 77
©St. Cross Features: 184
©Alain Dejean/Sygma: 71
©Abbie Rowe/White House, 1962: 10

All other photographs are from Michael Sellers' personal collection.

The authors and publisher have made every reasonable effort to contact all copyright holders. Any errors that may have occurred are inadvertent and anyone who for any reason has not been contacted is invited to write to the publisher so that a full acknowledgement may be made in subsequent editions of this work.